Ray of Hope

One man's dream. Hundreds served.

By Gary Lloyd

"As we have therefore opportunity, let us do good unto all men." --Galatians 6:10

Table of Contents

Prologue: A dream

Part 1

Chapter 1: A Beetle in the corridor

Chapter 2: His little girl

Chapter 3: Photographs

Chapter 4: A ministry is born

Chapter 5: Now that's church

Chapter 6: Happy as a lamb

Chapter 7: Popping wheelies

Chapter 8: He kept doing it

Chapter 9: Relentless

Chapter 10: God has provided

Chapter 11: Angels again

Part 2

Chapter 12: Cold-calling

Chapter 13: Dedicated and compassionate

Chapter 14: That ramp is a godsend

Chapter 15: They helped me a whole lot

Chapter 16: A blessing that can never be taken away

Chapter 17: They build with heart

Chapter 18: Like a kid going down a hill

Chapter 19: By the grace of God

Chapter 20: Led to help

Chapter 21: Good ol' country stuff

Chapter 22: I try to pray every day

Chapter 23: Not a dime

Chapter 24: A dream come true

Chapter 25: I'll call them angels

Chapter 26: Away we go

Chapter 27: Everybody helped everybody

Part 3

Chapter 28: No more powerful than that

Chapter 29: Five hundred

Epilogue: Galatians

Prologue: A dream

Sometimes, we overthink things. I know I have. Case in point: Back in the humid summer of 2016, I was facing somewhat of a dilemma. My second book had been published the previous winter, and I had just about put the finishing touches on my third. All that was left was to have a photographer friend of mine snap some photos and wade through the tedious design process. A lot was out of my hands during that time, waiting on touched-up pictures and proof copies to be mailed. So, I wondered, what should I write next? I had most recently put together two works of fiction and desired to make the jump back over to non-fiction, to tell something real, something that required me to interview people.

I anxiously and somewhat cynically scribbled down ideas. There was a baseball program, its culture positively changed by a focused and God-fearing head coach. That would not have made a book, most likely, but certainly a great long-form feature article. There was a high school football team, which overcame a few years of unthinkable adversity -- the state

Supreme Court saying it couldn't participate in the playoffs because of an ineligible team member, a player dying after an individual workout, a player's mom dying during the season, and more -- to finally claim a state championship. That could definitely have been a book, had I pursued it, and I still believe it is a story worth telling. I just wanted to tell something different.

There were other half-thought-out ideas. None seemed to have that "it" factor or depth that any book needs to transform from an outline to thousands of words. I wanted to write something important, meaningful, long-lasting. I was drawing blanks. It was staring me square in the face, and it took a Facebook post, of all things, for the light bulb in my mind to flick on.

It crossed my News Feed on June 6, 2016, late in the afternoon. It was a post my mother-in-law, Ramona Ray, had shared. It included two photos. One was of a long, wooden wheelchair ramp leading to a house, each plank covered by names, messages, and Bible verses written in green, purple and blue Magic Marker ink. The other was of a beautiful piece of craftsmanship, a wooden carving that read, "Ray of Hope

Ramp 500." Ramona commented above the post, "Jimmy's dream is still going strong! So thankful to everyone who has kept this ministry going! I'm pretty sure he's smiling down on this one!"

Jimmy Ray was Ramona's husband, my wife Jessica's father, and I never got the chance to meet him. He died before Jessica and I met in March 2012, a blind date at a spring carnival in Trussville, Alabama, where I broke entirely too many twenty-dollar bills trying to pop red balloons with blue-feathered darts to win Jessica a stuffed animal. It was either a monkey or bear. I struggled with spoken words, especially the emotional ones, so a few months later, in a May 31, 2012, letter, I told Jessica how I felt about her across a sheet of notebook paper in bright red ink. I intended to leave her Birmingham apartment before she read it. I didn't make it. She read it as I sat on her living room recliner, fidgeting my hands and trying not to sweat. Jessica later had that letter framed. What I did not know at the time was that she had penned her own letter to me on the exact same day, and she gave it to me on September 7, 2013, our wedding day in Chelsea, Alabama, at a picturesque wedding chapel a few miles off a busy highway, a true diamond in the rough. There was a spacious green lawn, browned farm fencing, a huge lake of blue where children littered the waves in green canoes, and a small pond just off the reception building. In part of that letter, Jessica eloquently wrote, "I have not told you yet, but I know already that I love you and that you will one day be my husband. I can't explain those feelings but the give and take, the comfort and stability, the little things of our relationship tell me that you and I will be the ones who make it." Beautiful. She had not known I was writing her a letter, declaring my feelings. I did not know that she was doing the same, on the same day. I suppose you call that fate. I keep that letter not in my wallet or SUV's center console, lest it get damaged. It stays in my nightstand in our bedroom, where I can always get to it. I read it from time to time, to reminisce, to ease my mind after a tough day.

    On our wedding day, my dad, Rick, graciously offered to walk Jessica down the aisle, but she respectfully declined, choosing to attach a small locket containing a photo of Jimmy to her bouquet of pearl-white flowers. My dad, of course, understood. At the wedding reception, there was a remembrance table in honor of Jimmy, so he was certainly there in spirit. The framed photo of him that sat on that table now rests on our living room mantle at home.

    I knew not a whole lot about Jimmy. I knew that he was a big man with an even bigger heart, and that he had dealt with serious health issues for quite some time. I knew, from Jessica, that he and I both sought out the Little League World Series on ESPN each August, to satisfy our sports entertainment craving until college football kicked off a few weeks later. I knew that our mannerisms were similar, and that we both patiently reacted to circumstances that should have ticked us off. Jimmy, my dad, my brother, David, and I would have had a blast together, I'm certain. We surely would have spent time on Jessica's grandparents' land in Andalusia, Alabama, casting lines from chrome-plated Zebco 33s into murky waters as the white goats munched on the tall grass behind us. We likely would have laughed about past experiences, discussed the plight of football's I-formation and dogged each other about who caught the biggest fish. I never catch the biggest fish.

I knew that Jimmy meant so much to Jessica and Ramona. That was obvious. He appeared in pictures in Ramona's home in Pace, Florida, in Jessica's Birmingham apartment and on her office desk. They talked about him and laughed. They talked about him and cried. Jessica and Ramona spend days, like his birthday, July 31, and February 28, the day he died, together, going to lunch, movies and parks. I'm not sure what all they talk about, but I'm sure there is more laughter, more tears. They visit his gravesite at Elizabeth Chapel Church Cemetery in Chumuckla, Florida, and arrange the prettiest flowers they can find. I have observed all these situations. Each time, I am reminded that life is way too short, that each life should be spent making the most of it for others.

This book is not about loss and sadness and grief at all, really. It is about a man's dream, how he came up with that dream, how he turned it into reality, and how that dream is still a reality every day, even all these years after his death. It is an important book, I believe, the most important words I have ever typed across a bright computer screen under a crimson wall of framed press passes that got me into Bryant-Denny Stadium in Tuscaloosa for free, next to mounds of notebooks in which I scrawled out words about cold-blooded murders, house fires that consumed everything, teenagers who courageously battled rare forms of cancer, football games I do not remember attending. Writing this book, I got a chance to know my father-in-law. I was fortunate enough to learn about his heart through the words of others, who laughed one moment and got choked up the next as they talked about him. Now my parents, brother, and other relatives can know him, too. It will give Jessica and Ramona something to hold onto, something tangible to clutch tight when they are feeling sentimental and want to recall the impact Jimmy had on his corner of the world. Maybe Jessica will keep it in her desk drawer at her office in Birmingham and flip through some pages when she is having a bad day, or on her nightstand in late February and late July, as those anniversary dates approach. Maybe Ramona will keep it in her purse as she drives south to Chumuckla to visit Jimmy's grave, or within arm's reach of her living room recliner. Maybe having his story so close by will ease their minds in the difficult times. I hope it does. Our children will be able to develop a connection to a grandfather they will never meet through the words of his family and friends, the words printed herein.

      Many people across this country, across the world, have heard of or know someone like Jimmy, someone who put his or her own wants and needs aside to come to the aid of others, the less fortunate. In my time as a journalist, I have learned that those stories are increasingly difficult to find in a Tweet-centric world. We care about headlines, who is dating who in Hollywood, which group was offended by what statement, one-hundred-forty characters of information that have no real relevance to us or others. These days, we care about sensationalized headlines and driving traffic to news websites, no matter the impact such stories have on people's lives. It can be maddening, if you allow it to consume you.

There should and always will be a place for the stories that truly matter, whether it be a three-minute feature in a two-hour college football preview show on a major television network, four pages in a sixty-eight-page magazine, or one book that is not even resting on an aisle with a thousand others at the Barnes and Noble. Those stories are the true needles in the haystack, and I wish that was not the case. I wish they earned more air time, more layout space in magazines, more copies on the shelves. I wish we could silence the cell phones and mash the Sleep button on the iPad. I wish instant communication among children meant pedaling a red Huffy down the street to meet, not frantically searching for just the right emoji to send in a text message. I wish we truly experienced the moments of our lives, instead of filtering them on Instagram. Really, I just wish we would slow down a little bit, and maybe do something nice for someone else, something as simple as holding a door open for someone six steps behind you. Little gestures can change someone's mood in an instant. It can help them through the next hour, or even the entire day. It can inspire them to pay it forward, and before you know it, each customer is paying for the chicken sandwiches and nuggets for the car behind them in the Chick-fil-A drive-thru, shoppers are taking the five extra seconds to hold the door open for the slower gentleman with a cane, boxes of candy are being left in mailboxes for hardworking postal workers during the Christmas season. In this book's case, one wheelchair ramp constructed for someone in need becomes one hundred, then two hundred, then more than five hundred.

    What an impact. What a legacy. And it all started with thinking about others.

Part 1

Chapter 1: A Beetle in the corridor

When Jimmy Ray was about seven-and-a-half years old, in March 1962, he pulled an electric coffee pot off a table and onto himself, scalding his skin. The accident resulted in second- and third-degree burns on his chest and belly. It left scars, scars that always seemed to embarrass him years later. He would never be without a shirt after that, even at a pool or in the waters of the Gulf of Mexico.

"Even though it must have been excruciating, I never saw him cry," says his older sister, Sharon Ray Glover.

Sharon's words could be left to pertain to that memory, and that memory alone, stuck in time like a fly in honey. But her words transcend just sizzling coffee. In a lot of ways, they define his lifetime.

*****

Jimmy was the baby of four children, born July 31, 1954, in Portsmouth, Ohio. His three siblings were Jerry, born in 1945; Sharon, born in 1948; and Barbara, born in 1952. He grew up in Milton, Florida, a short drive over Escambia Bay away from Pensacola.

"Jimmy was the cutest little brother," Sharon says. "I can't remember him getting in trouble. Except for one time, my dad brought home a go-cart in the back seat of the car. He told Barbara and Jimmy not to touch it until he got it out."

Instead, Jimmy talked Barbara into helping him take the go-cart out of the car. When their father came outside and saw what had happened, Jimmy told Barbara to run, thinking he would stay behind and earn the punishment in full. But Barbara's running made their father even madder, so he chased her and spanked her. Jimmy got off scot-free.

The closest that Jimmy came to getting in big trouble was when he was sixteen or seventeen years old as a student at historic Milton High School.

"It was probably a dare," Sharon remembers.

Ramona Aughtman, who later became Jimmy's wife, went to Pace High School, but she remembers the story well.

Jimmy was not a rebel, but he did not really care what people thought of him. He enjoyed himself. He drove a dark green Volkswagen Beetle, maybe a

1964 or 1965 model. The school's classrooms were built in single rows facing the outside with wide sidewalk corridors, with iron posts on the outside holding up an awning. One day, some of his classmates dared him to drive that Beetle through one of the narrow outdoor corridors of the school. The corridor, of course, was cleared, so that no one was in danger. There also had to be lookouts for teachers and administrators. Jimmy did not hesitate. He maneuvered his car into one end of the corridor and quickly sped out the other.

"He was always up for a dare," Ramona says. "He would do stuff like that. He just enjoyed life."

Ramona and Jimmy started off being friends. It grew from there. He was a good person, stable, and she could trust him, quality traits that everyone looks for in a partner.

"He fit the bill," she says. "He was easy to talk to."

Over the course of their growing relationship, the two became close, as all couples do. One knew what the other was thinking. They could finish each other's sentences. They were married on July 16, 1976.

Thinking back today on those early years together, a memory pops into Ramona's head. She remembers the first time she met Jimmy's mother. The words Jimmy's mother spoke to her still resonate today.

"He has a heart as big as all outdoors," Jimmy's mother said.

Chapter 2: His little girl

The beauty is in the simplicity.
There are no extravagant trips to the mega castle at Disney World in Orlando, or seats on the fifty-yard line at Ben Hill Griffin Stadium at the University of Florida campus in Gainesville. There is no tall stack of VHS tapes for the young girl to sit and watch all day. After all, she would rather be outside playing. There are no absurdly expensive toys or games for the girl to play with in the floor. After all, she would rather play with her daddy.

He was scared to death of her to begin with, afraid he would break the small blue-eyed girl who was born on June 14, 1988. Jimmy and Ramona were married for twelve years before having their first child. There was a miscarriage three months before getting pregnant again. He had wanted a son, someone to throw the ball with in the back yard. All expectant fathers wish for that, at least a little bit, but they are ultimately over-the-moon happy regardless of their baby's gender.

"He was as happy as he could be with his little girl," Ramona says.

He loved to sit in the recliner with her, her head resting on his chest. She would hold her head up and jabber away, and he would just sit and listen. Over time, the fear of breaking the child faded. He would lie in the floor and play with her, pushing cars across a blanket embroidered with streets. He would insert a rope through a cardboard box and drag her up and down the hallway. She always loved that.

The date on the recording is May of 1989, when the young girl, named Jessica, is not quite one year old. Jimmy is lying on the floor with his baby girl, who had been born the previous June. She is having a ball, piling laundry -- towels, socks, shirts, anything she can get her hands on -- on her dad.

In a June 1989 home video, Jimmy is again lying down, this time in the back yard grass at the Ray family home on Charles Circle in Pace, Florida. The house is small, three bedrooms, one bathroom, built by Ramona's father decades ago. The aluminum roof, front porch columns and shutters are all forest green, the bricks painted white. The three towering trees in the front yard twist high above the power lines and into the sky, a gray squirrel's dream. The property the house sits on is spacious and flat, stretching deep into the beginnings of shallow woods, mostly a thicket of bamboo. In the fall, when the green leaves have fallen from the live oak trees and cover the lawn, Pace High School is even more visible from the back yard, just beyond a wide field of white cotton. In that back yard in June 1989, nestled close to another large tree, is a plastic kiddie pool. Jessica is splashing around and dumping water from a plastic cup as the family dog, Killer, drinks from the pool. Jimmy is lying in the grass, and each time Jessica dumps the water back into the pool, Jimmy is right there to fill the cup back up. Eventually, Jessica climbs out of the pool and decides to wander the perimeter of the back yard. Jimmy holds her hand, helping her to get to each destination she points to.

    A year later, in April 1990, Jimmy is shoveling a heap of dirt from the back of his small Chevrolet truck into the yard, for a project that cannot be determined. He has enough brown dirt to fill in a roadside ditch. Suffice it to say, he clearly has a lot of work ahead of him. Jessica, not quite two years old, is outside helping, using her red plastic shovel and yellow rake to sort through the dirt. Later that day, Jimmy is underneath his green Rally riding lawnmower, changing out the metal blades. Jessica is again by his side, peeking underneath the lawnmower's deck and handing her daddy the old wrenches that he needs. When she peers underneath, Jimmy makes sure to shield her face from coming too close to the blades.

In a February 10, 1991 home movie, there is no laundry to be refolded after Jessica covers Jimmy with it, no plastic kiddie pool to fill with water from a garden hose, no yard work to complete. There is only a blue swing in a park. Jessica, dressed in all pink, continues to put one foot on one side of the swing and one on the other. Jimmy steps in and shows her how to sit on the swing, where to hold on, how to keep her feet up as she glides back and forth through the air. As she rocks to and fro, she smiles.

Four months later, when Jessica is almost three years old, she is back in that plastic kiddie pool, splashing water all around. She has always been drawn to water, to pools, to the beach. Ramona is filming. Jimmy is sitting on a flipped-over five-gallon bucket, his jeans rolled up to his knees, his feet submerged in the cool water. He holds a plastic toy watering can, which he fills with water to dump on his young daughter. Jessica squeals and laughs when this happens. She begins to splash him with water. The two play back and forth, flinging water on each other. At one point, Jessica gets water in her blue eyes. She trudges over to Jimmy, who says that he is sorry. She presses her face to his blue shirt, and he dries her eyes. It is a nice moment between father and daughter. The duel appears to be over. Then, just as Jessica pulls away from her dad's shirt, she splashes him again. He splashes right back. This goes on and on and on. He does not get bored playing this simple game with his daughter. In fact, it does not appear he could be much happier. After what feels like half an hour, Jimmy is soaked, his light blue shirt now darkened. He looks toward the camera, laughing. Ramona says, "Just remember, you started this," and laughs. It appears this fun could continue until the kiddie pool is completely out of water.

In November of 1991, Jimmy returns home in his navy blue Chevrolet truck with eight to ten pieces of lumber. Jessica fiddles with them on the ground in front of their house. Jimmy uses a hammer, metal with a black rubber handle, to build a structure. Jessica, of course, beats on the nail heads her daddy just nailed into the lumber with a plastic red hammer. Ramona asks Jessica if she has a "woman hammer" and what kind Jimmy is using. "A man one," she replies. The home video then cuts to December 7, 1991. It is dark outside their home, lit only by the manger scene that Jimmy built with the lumber.

One of the final home videos is from May 17, 1992, when Jessica is nearing her fourth birthday. She is again in the back yard playing in the water, this time a sprinkler. Jimmy places his hand in the streams of water, sending it everywhere. Jessica then picks up the sprinkler and chases Jimmy around the yard with it. At one point, Jessica stops and just holds the sprinkler. She is not paying attention to Jimmy, who sneaks up behind her, takes the sprinkler, and chases her with it.

Sometime between Jessica's sixth and eighth birthdays, she found out that her dad was sick. While Jessica stayed at her grandparents' house in Pace, Jimmy found out from the doctor that he had congestive heart failure. Jessica remembers the doctor giving him maybe six to eight more years to live. He had other health issues he was battling. Blood did not circulate well in his legs. He battled asbestosis, a result of the inhalation of asbestos particles. He dealt with glaucoma, which led to losing a good bit of his vision in one eye. He had nagging arthritis in his knees. Everyday activities such as walking, driving, and working were difficult and painful. Did he complain?

"No," Jessica says succinctly. "Never."

Chapter 3: Photographs

The album is made of criss-crossed dark brown leather, and it is thick, maybe a couple inches. There are fifty pages inside, each with clear sleeves on their fronts and backs. Forty-six of these pages are filled with photos, all of Jimmy. The album rested on its own cubby hole of our television stand in our first home in Birmingham, Alabama, not long after Jessica and I got married. After a year there, we moved to Moody, Alabama, and that photo album took its rightful spot when all the boxes were unpacked. I have flipped through those forty-six pages several times, to learn as much as I could about Jimmy, about his interests and personality. The photo album provides quite the glimpse.

A photo of Jimmy graces its cover, his grin ever so slight, his hair vaguely windblown, the sleeves of his baby-blue button-down shirt rolled up to his elbows. It is not clear what he is doing, if he has been raking leaves, casting a spinnerbait into brownish-green water or simply posing for a photograph. But he looks happy.

The first page of the album immediately makes you laugh. The top photo shows Jimmy with his tongue halfway sticking out of his mouth, his eyes pinched shut. He looks as if he has taken a huge bite out of a lemon or swallowed an enormous gulp of apple cider vinegar. On the back of that first page, there is a picture of Jimmy as a young boy, perhaps a school picture. His hair is short and combed to the right. His cheeks and nose are freckled, and he has not quite grown into his ears. Just above that photo is one of Jimmy as an adult, standing in front of a glistening small lake or pond. He has a leash in each hand, both attached to two teeny dogs, probably just puppies at the time.

The next several pages paint a clear picture of Jimmy's hobbies. In one photo, he is standing on the bank of a pond, holding a two-feet-long catfish. In another, he is sitting in his recliner, loading ammunition into his Winchester Model 94 twelve-gauge shotgun. He sits in the same recliner a page later, and his hands are full. He holds a fishing rod in one hand, a new box of fishing lures tucked under his right arm. In his left hand, he holds a Roland Martin instructional video on how to customize your helicopter lure. In an obvious flow of cause and effect, the picture immediately following Jimmy's new gifts is of him sitting in a white lawn chair, a catfish hooked on the line.

Most of the photos in the album follow this pattern. They show a man in his element, content with his hobbies and the simplicities of life. There is a photo of him hammering together a small deck, spinning a blue yo-yo, casting that helicopter lure from muddy banks, rolling in the grass with his dogs, sitting beside a campfire, posing in a navy blue cowboy hat. There are photos of Jimmy holding his newborn daughter, blowing bubbles with her in the back yard, nudging yellow backhoes and dump trucks across a sandbox, cavorting in a small fort made from a Mickey Mouse blanket, lounging in the slope in a road of sand that has filled with water, helping a smiling Jessica up the metal stairs and down the aluminum slide at a playground. The photos of the father and daughter seem to get better as Jessica gets older. She fishes with him, helping to reel in a small bass. She sits in her own kid-sized lawn chair as he casts from his. She makes birthday cake batter in a bowl for her mom's birthday while sitting on the kitchen counter, Jimmy standing close by. They play putt-putt together, Jimmy keeping score.

    The entirety of this album takes on a carefree personality, chronicling moments of day trips to fish, fun times in the back yard. There never appears to be worry, frustration or any semblance of despair. There is, however, one photo that does not seem to belong. It is on the forty-fifth page, and the timestamp shows that it is from December 16, 2003. It is of Jimmy sitting behind a wooden desk, surrounded by mounds of paperwork and metal file cabinets. He has a pen in his right hand, and his left index finger runs down a sheet of paper. He is intensely focused. He is clearly working on something he has a deep passion for.

Chapter 4: A ministry is born

It was sometime in the 1990s, the exact year Ramona cannot remember. But she and Jimmy were driving down the road when they passed a mobile home where the residents were trying to use an old plywood ramp, buckled and warped, pretty much useless, to help a person who used a wheelchair out.

"He said to me, 'If I had the money I would build them a decent ramp that they could use,'" Ramona remembers. "And it wouldn't be out of plywood, either."

Jimmy had strong feelings opposing inferior workmanship. He possessed a desire to use the right materials. No matter the job, it had to be done right. Where his passion for helping people in wheelchairs came from, Ramona does not know. No one in their immediate family was in one at the time. It had to be a God-given desire, she says.

A few years later, Jimmy learned of a man in Pensacola that had built wheelchair ramps for a couple people. He saw it on the Channel 3 news. Jimmy repeated his desire to build ramps for people who needed them. So, he did. Ramona and Jessica were his assistants. They used their own money, their own slim resources, to complete the projects. Ramona remembers working in the rain, heat and cold.

"But no matter how hot or tired we were, by the time we finished the ramp we were always blessed far more than the ones who received the ramp," Ramona says. "Funny how God works that way."

Jimmy's passion for those in need and quality craftsmanship was apparent. There were eleven general requirements for handicap ramps, according to Jimmy. The first was that frames and runners were to be made up of two-by-six material. Four-by-four posts were to be set five feet apart and cemented two feet in the ground. Deck runners were to be no more than two feet apart, and the ramps would be four feet wide. Two-by-six supports were to be placed under the runners at each post. The handrail posts were to be cut thirty-four inches high from the top of the deck board. The top handrail would be made up of two-by-four material. The deck board would be made of 5/4-inch wood nailed to and beneath the top handrail, and it would also be used for the bottom cane rail and middle rail. Ramps exceeding thirty feet in length required a rest platform. And, finally, ramps were required to be built to not drop more than one inch for every foot of length.

Ramps were built for people who did not have the money. They could not afford a ramp, but certainly were in need of one. Jimmy would contact a nearby social services organization that knew of elderly people in need of wheelchair ramps, and he would begin his work. It began with measuring how wide the ramp needed to be, and how much slope there was from the top of the front door to the ground. That helped in determining how much lumber would be needed, and how high the ramp would need to be.

"There is no way to explain when you do something for someone who can't pay you back, there is just a sense of satisfaction I think God gives you," Ramona says.

It quickly became apparent that the family of three could not afford to keep Jimmy's passion for building ramps alive. But he wanted to keep it going. No, he had to keep it going.

"I believe some people are just born with that ability," Ramona says. "It's kind of like a spiritual gift that God gives certain people, and I believe He gave that one to Jimmy. He just had the ability to kind of see or discern that people had certain needs."

The trio needed help. It came from a church family.

"I think if he hadn't found those people when he did, or God hadn't brought him to those people and them to him, I don't think it would have continued too terribly much longer," says Jessica, Jimmy's daughter. "It was to that point where it had outgrown us. We couldn't keep up with that for much longer."

During this time, the Ray family had begun attending Woodbine United Methodist Church in Pace. At the time, the youth director, Ronnie Calvert, was setting up service projects. Jimmy mentioned to him the need for wheelchair ramps in the community.

"I wanted to do some sort of mission week during the summer with the youth, and Jimmy and I came up with the idea to build ramps for the needy," Ronnie says. "We would also paint houses during those mission weeks as well."

The church funded the projects. After a few ramps were built, the youth members of the church excitedly told their parents about what they had been doing. The parents wanted to know more, so they began to come to the ramp builds as well.

"We did that for two or three summers before the men of Woodbine took it over," Ronnie says.

Those days building wheelchair ramps with the youth kickstarted a new ministry. Quickly, the projects went from hammers, skill saws and post-hole diggers to nail guns, table saws and augers. There was even a trailer to hold all the equipment.

The ministry was growing because people saw the need, and Jimmy was never bashful about asking people for help, telling them why this was so important. He could sell ice to an eskimo. By the time he was through talking with someone about the ministry, they were pulling out their wallets, asking him how much he needed.

Says volunteer David Boyd, "He never said anything but the truth, but you were moved to help in any way you could, to pay for things to help these people."

To lead off a Woodbine United Methodist Church Missions & Outreach Ministry August 2005 newsletter, Jimmy chose a devotional from F.B. Meyer's book, "Our Daily Walk." It was headed with Galatians 6:10, which states, "As we have therefore opportunity, let us do good unto all men." The one-page devotional describes three methods of helping people, as indicated by the Apostle Paul: The restoration of the fallen, the care of pastors and ministers, and the ministry of all men. It describes how everyone has a mission in the world, though we may never be called to cross the sea or visit distant lands to preach the gospel. Christ's command to each of us begins with the person next to us, to not wait to be neighbored, but to neighbor somebody who is in need. The best way to bring in the Kingdom of God is to bring the person whom you can most easily influence to the Savior, it says. All great work in the world has commenced, not by committees, but by the consecration, self-sacrifice, and devotion of single individuals.

The newsletter ends with a prayer: "Give us grace to be

encouragers of others, never discouragers; always making life easier, never harder, for those who come within our influence. Amen."

Chapter 5: Now that's church

Billy Pittman is a jack of all trades. He has worked various jobs, all blue-collar work with hands so strong that a leisurely handshake pinches nerves and pops knuckles. He has been a painter, removed and retextured ceilings, run a chainsaw, repaired stucco and drywall, done light plumbing and carpentry work, installed interior doors and hurricane shutters, put up fencing, built pergolas and wheelchair ramps. He has done a little bit of everything. One time, when a couple could not affix a new ceiling fan in a living room themselves because of their arms tiring and repeatedly dropping small screws to the floor, Billy put the fan up all by himself. He held it above his head with one hand and used a screwdriver with the other. A man like that was a dream for Jimmy's wheelchair ramp ministry. They met for the first time when Jimmy's truck ran hot, and Billy came over to fix it. Their friendship grew from there, and from building ramps together as part of Woodbine's outreach program.

Their relationship revolved around joking with each other. Jimmy loved Dodge trucks and drove an old white one at the time. Billy drove a Ford. After building a ramp on the northern end of Santa Rosa County, Jimmy got his truck stuck in the slick mud. The tires just spun. Billy was there in his red Ford truck. He hooked up a rope to Jimmy's truck and pulled him out. A picture was taken, proving that Ford was indeed the better model. Once the Dodge was pulled out of the mud, Jimmy told Billy, "I told you this Dodge could push that Ford with a rope."

"He could spin it to make it funny," Billy says.

Billy assisted on many ramp builds as a volunteer, so many that he can no longer remember most of them. They run together in his mind. But one in particular stands out. It was, of course, the first build he was a part of, on a hot Saturday in July. The ramp was for a boy with cerebral palsy, about ten years old, who struggled to walk. He lived in a mobile home, which sat about thirty-six to forty inches off the ground. While volunteers constructed the ramp, Stan Holmes, one of the volunteers, went swimming with the boy at his home's pool.

"That was really cool," Billy says.

The day only got better. Billy carried a huge barbecue grill on his trailer and hauled it an hour east to Ponce de Leon Springs State Park. The boy and his family came, too. Because it was a state park, there was an entry fee. When the gatekeepers were told what the group had done, the whole group got in for free. The ministry brought a load of chicken, barbecue and sausage. Jimmy was always the one to feed the volunteers, to cook sausage in the morning before the work began, to order the pizzas after. Billy set up his grill inside the park and cooked all the meat. People who were at the park fishing, hiking, birding, and swimming saw, and smelled, what was going on. There were a hundred chicken leg quarters, not to mention the sausage links, barbecue and potato salad. There was so much food, it was as if the ministry was catering for the park. People there were slow to come up to the group, but when a few started to trickle toward all that food, more and more came. They were looking for "the catch," what they had to do or sign up for or pay to get some food. There was no catch. The group had more than enough food, so it passed out full plates all afternoon.

"Jimmy was in his element there," Billy says. "That is what Jimmy did. That is who he was."

When the final piece of chicken left the grill, no one else came through the line, and not because the food had run out. There was no one in the park left who had not eaten. The amount of food the group brought was just enough for a park full of people.

"It just worked out where the last piece of chicken hit the plate to serve somebody, everybody was served," Billy says.

The group had not planned out how much meat to buy. It just worked out that it was enough for the number of people in the park that afternoon.

"God knew what we needed, and that is exactly what we had," Billy says.

David Boyd was there that day, and he remembers the three words Jimmy uttered just after that last person walked off with a plate of food.

"Now that's church," he said.

Chapter 6: Happy as a lamb

The man's plan was so troubling, so sad, that something had to be done.

His name was Robert, and he was a double amputee confined to a wheelchair. His plan, if his home were ever to catch fire, was to roll toward the front door, open it, fall out of the chair, and roll himself out of the house to safety. It sounds as if it could be a joke, but one look at the man describing his plan in a 2005 interview lets you know just how serious he was.

Robert was bound inside his home since sometime in 2002, unable to exit through the front door. He had no wheelchair ramp, no way to get out of his house to check for the mail, to say hello to the neighbors, to water the white and pink flowers that lined the perimeter of his home. He was stuck.

The local ABC television news affiliate in the Pensacola area, Channel 3, ran a story about Jimmy's wheelchair ramp ministry on April 4, 2005. It was part of the affiliate's "Angels in our Midst" segment, which highlights good people doing positive things in various communities. Robert was the recipient of the ministry's fifty-third ramp. The interview opens with Jimmy talking about the ministry. He says that he never realized that there were hundreds of people that could not get out of their homes without somebody coming over to help them.

"And that's ... that's not right," Jimmy says in the interview, subtly shaking his head. In that brief moment, it is obvious that Jimmy is bothered by this, that providing a way out for people in wheelchairs is his mission. It clearly means a lot to him.

According to the story, Robert's social worker contacted the Woodbine United Methodist Church group and explained that Robert was in danger, that he could not leave his home. Jimmy and his team of volunteers were on site to build a wheelchair ramp within two days.

"I was about the happiest man in the world," Robert says in the interview. "I was happy, just as happy as a lamb. I could get out of the house."

The ramp was not the only surprise for Robert the day his ramp was constructed. He had been confined to a manual wheelchair. However, he was also presented with a new motorized wheelchair. In the interview, Robert says that he could not hardly stand it because he did not know what to say.

"He started smiling, and I don't think he stopped until we left," Jimmy says in the interview.

Near the end of the video story, Robert's social worker states that the group changed his life forever. Robert says that he can go outside, around the flower-lined red house and into the back yard. His smile is infectious.

Jimmy's voice plays over a scene of Robert wheeling around his front yard. He says, "To see their faces and stuff when (the ramps) are done, it just makes it all worthwhile."

Chapter 7: Popping wheelies

They often sat in the shade and talked.

Tyler was mostly non-verbal but could get his point across when he wanted to, and Jimmy quickly learned to understand him. Tyler was born with a genetic disease, Lesch-Nyhan, which presents itself much like cerebral palsy, but has other issues, such as self-abusive tendencies. If he got excited, Tyler would need his hands and feet restrained, to keep him from harming himself or those near him. Because of the self-harming aspects of Tyler's disability, he could not have a motorized chair for regular use.

"He did have one that we used much like a child has a battery-operated car," Tyler's mother, Ann, says. "He loved chasing us around and going in circles with it."

Ann met Jimmy shortly after coming to Woodbine United Methodist Church in the spring of 2008.

"Such a kind man, and so full of God's spirit," she says.

Ann says that she, her husband and Tyler started volunteering with the ramp ministry because they knew of the need firsthand.

"Some would talk to him, but Jimmy would get Tyler to interact," she says. "Jimmy never treated Tyler as if he were different. He would go over to Tyler and ask him to keep him company while the others did the work, and I'm sure they shared a story or two while sitting there."

After ramp builds, Jimmy always ordered pizza for lunch for the volunteers. He quickly learned that Tyler loved pizza.

"I would hear a squeal from my son when they decided it was time to order the pizza," Ann says.

Tyler would also "test drive" the ramps when they were completed. The volunteers would talk to him and joke with him.

"It was not only a great experience for Tyler, but as a mom it meant the world to me," Ann says.

Ann says that the house her family lives in has just two steps, so they were just "popping wheelies" with Tyler's wheelchair to get him in and out of the house. One day, unknown to Ann, someone measured the front of her house for a metal plating ramp and installed it while the family was not at home.

"Such a blessing to us," she says.

Ann went on many ramp builds. She helped Ramona cook breakfast for the volunteers. She even joked that they would rather have her handle a spatula than a nail gun.

"I would love to listen to all the volunteers -- men, women and children -- talk about how they were going to be blessed today," Ann says.

Ann remembers one ramp build in particular. It was built on Christmas Eve, for a little boy who was about five years old. The group showed up at nine o'clock in the morning to build the ramp. Another of the church's ministries supplied Christmas dinner and gifts for the children.

"It was pouring rain, but we all smiled and worked through it," Ann says. "I can still see the little boy in his chair and his sister standing there watching us through the storm door."

A family member distracted the children so the gifts could be smuggled inside.

"There were smiles, hugs and an overall peace at that house that day that would not have happened had God not destined Ray of Hope into Jimmy's mind and heart," Ann says.

Twenty months later, Tyler passed away. He was eighteen years old, an age he reached just two weeks prior to his death. He came home from school not feeling well. Ann had ordered the pizza that he loved so much, but he did not want it. All he wanted to do was watch television in his room. Ann placed him in his bed and turned on the television. She checked on him many times, asking if he wanted a drink or the pizza. Each time he said no. That night, while Ann was at Bible study with her husband and Tyler's dad stayed with him, Tyler passed away. His memorial service drew more than two hundred people.

"I found out so many things about my son that I didn't know from all those that spoke," Ann says. "He was well loved and such a blessing to all that knew him."

Since his passing, Tyler's family has donated his metal plating ramp back to Ray of Hope to be used for someone else's ramp.

"The ramp ministry has blessed my family in so many ways," Ann says. "It's more than supplying a ramp. They are part of my family."

Chapter 8: He kept doing it

Jimmy's health was worsening. It quickly reached the point where he could no longer help build the wheelchair ramps, and that was tough. Imagine realizing your dream, your calling in life, and when you are at the height of that calling, it is taken from you. Jimmy stayed as connected as he could. He began to work the phones. He would call the guys at Woodbine and tell them a ramp was needed here for a young boy and there for an elderly lady. For a while, Jimmy was able to go with the guys and sit in his "supervisor's chair" and offer advice on how the ramps should be built, and to make sure they put in the "kickers," which were boards placed underneath the ramp to add another level of support. Jimmy was quite particular about the kickers. Occasionally, the Monday after a ramp build on Saturday, he would call Billy Pittman to tell him that he knew those kickers were not all where they were supposed to be, so he would ask Billy to run by and add some more.

"These guys will never know how grateful Jimmy and I were to them for going out of their way to come pick up Jimmy and his chair so he could still be a part of the ministry he loved so much," Ramona says.

The time soon came when Jimmy was no longer able to go with them on ramp builds. The strain of tagging along was too much for him physically, taking him days to recover. It was not just the congestive heart failure that was an issue. After some ramp builds, he would come home and cry because he was in so much pain from the arthritis in his knees. Just standing up was painful. David Boyd had problems with his feet, and one time, on the way back home, they both just cried during the drive. He was disappointed, but he did not let it depress him. He continued to do what he could from home, which included taking requests for ramps, drawing up the plans for them, estimating the amount of materials needed, and then ordering them.

"He kept doing it," Ramona says.

Jimmy had been in charge of the measuring for each project, and that duty fell to Billy Pittman, Stan Holmes, Mark Sopris, Ed Lutes, and Jon Twitchell.

"Jimmy was forever telling me how grateful he was to these men and how he hated to constantly ask them to do this for him," Ramona says. "But they were so gracious and never complained."

He was grateful, of course, but he often told Ramona that he wished he could do more than just sit and watch. David Boyd remembers Jimmy's health beginning to break down. He saw him once a week, and he recalls Jimmy playing it cool.

"He never really let on how sick he was," David says.

*****

In the summer of 2009, Jessica graduated cum laude from the University of Florida with a bachelor's degree in family, youth and community sciences. She minored in nonprofit organizational leadership. Her parents trekked more than three hundred miles for her graduation, set to take place in the O'Connell Center, where the Gators host their college basketball games. The night before graduation, Jimmy and Ramona gave Jessica a necklace. It was her birthstone, a pearl, with a graduation cap. It included her initials and the graduation date. Inscribed on the back was, "You're the first, and we are so proud of you, with all our love, Mom and Dad." Also included is Proverbs 16:3: "Commit to the Lord whatever you do, and He will establish your plans." Jessica does not recall what she got for Christmas later that year, so this is the last gift she remembers receiving from her dad. She wears it all the time.

Chapter 9: Relentless

Ramona's parents had moved to Andalusia, Alabama, not far from Pace, Florida, off a winding dirt road. Their land is a postcard of country living. There are a couple dogs that roam their land, chasing squirrels up into the trees. There are many chickens and goats everywhere. There is a small lake down from the house's front door, with a pier that extends about twenty feet out over the blue water. A golf cart ride away is another circular pond, where Jimmy and Jessica often went fishing. Some goats would gnaw on the tall grass behind them as they casted lines attached to rubber purple worms and red bobbers. There were also cows that would come down to the pond to cool off, chasing the fish away. It was January 25, 2010, and Ramona and Jimmy were there for Ramona's mom's birthday. Jimmy did not feel well on that trip. He continued to feel bad during the following week. A doctor's appointment was scheduled for early February. Jimmy went to the doctor's appointment and was admitted into the hospital that day.

He did not wallow or complain. In fact, he was relentless. He was not relentless in his fight against his health issues. He understood that his health was failing, and that he might not live much longer. His energy was, of course, focused on the wheelchair ramp ministry. His plan was to have Stan Holmes take over for him.

"The memory of his constant chatter on our drive to the hospital for the last time will forever be burned into my memory," Ramona says. "He was so weak and would get completely out of breath trying to tell me all the details."

Jessica had already moved to Birmingham, Alabama, for her first post-college job. One night during Jimmy's hospital stay, his defibrillator went off, shocking him. The harder the shock, the more electricity it takes to start the heart back up. When this would happen at home, Jimmy would pass out just before the defibrillator fired. He would not feel the shock because he was unconscious. But this time, he did not pass out. He was asleep when the defibrillator fired and had dreamed that he had been shot by a bullet from a gun. Jimmy, up until this point, continued to make phone calls, design ramps, and order necessary supplies for the wheelchair ramp ministry.

"I think it's like anything else that you love to do," Jessica says. "As long as you're able to do it, you're going to do it. I think it gave him something else to focus on. He wasn't 'Woe is me.' It was never that."

Ramona made the decision to call Jessica without Jimmy's knowledge, because he didn't realize his time was as near as it was. He thought that as long as his defibrillator was firing, he would be alive for a while longer. Jessica began the four-hour drive at seven o'clock that night. She arrived after intensive care unit visiting hours were over, and those hours were strict: thirty minutes each, four times per day and no more than two visitors in the room at once. But the nurses let her see her father.

While in the intensive care unit, Jimmy was put on dialysis in the hopes of taking some of the stress off his kidneys, which were beginning to fail. The dialysis would either help or cause more kidney damage. There was no status quo. Jimmy opted for dialysis in hopes of having a little more time with Ramona and Jessica, but it wasn't meant to be. The dialysis failed and caused more damage, which is when the doctors told Ramona and Jessica that palliative care was the only option. Jimmy then went to hospice care.

Jessica could still feel his positivity. Sure, behind closed doors with Ramona, she believes there was probably some fear, some tears.

"But he knew where he was going," Jessica says. "He knew what he had done. He wanted to make sure it was left in good hands and that they knew what they were doing and how to do it."

During that hospital stay, visitors came in bunches. Jessica did not know a lot of them. Some said they had spoken to him on the phone about wheelchair ramps, about acquiring donations, more. At one point, Billy Pittman worried that he and others were visiting too much, if they were taking too much time away from Jessica and Ramona.

"People just loved him so much that people wanted to go see him, talk with him," Billy says. "Jimmy really enjoyed people coming by there and seeing him."

David Boyd remembers Jimmy struggling to breathe, but he was always thinking of others. Jimmy talked about how he wished he could have done more, how he desired to build more wheelchair ramps for those in need.

"What a testimony," David says. "He changed our outlook on life. It was the love of Christ flowing through Jimmy. Our lives were changed."

At one point during Jimmy's hospital stay, a group of boys and girls from the Nease (Florida) High School ROTC program passed through Pensacola on its way to New Orleans. Along its trip, which the group had made for the previous several years, it stopped to do service projects in Pensacola. Mostly, the group picked up litter off the sandy beaches.

"That's kind of like fishing in the ocean," Stan Holmes says. "You could pick up litter at the beach for the rest of your life, and you are never going to see the difference, really."

The group's master sergeant got in touch with the wheelchair ramp ministry of Woodbine United Methodist Church. The boys and girls were going to stop and help build four ramps in one day. They were also going to venture to the Ray home in Pace, to clean up the yard and whatever else they could do. It was rainy on the Saturday the boys came. Jimmy had manned the phones, ordering lumber, calling Stan to make sure there were doughnuts in the morning and pizza in the afternoon for all twenty-two of the boys who made the trip. He did this all from his hospital bed.

"All he could think of is, 'Who are we going to build for? How are we going to take care of these teenagers? What kind of impact can we have on their lives?' That was just the way Jimmy Ray did it," Stan says.

All options were exhausted in that hospital room. Doctors just could not get the built-up fluid off and away from Jimmy's heart. He did not wish to go home, to leave behind the memory of his passing within those walls. Jimmy was feeling a bit better his first day at the hospice care facility. The antibiotics were getting out of his system. Billy Pittman remembers that day, because there was barbecue catered at his place of employment. There was way too much. He brought pans of barbecue to the facility and, with Ramona's blessing, took some to Jimmy. He lit up. His diet had eliminated salts and anything that made him retain fluid. But, now in hospice care, he could pretty much have whatever he wanted.

Jessica remembers there being talk of how patients can only stay in hospice thirty days before needing to go somewhere else. She remembers Jimmy being certain that he would surpass that thirty-day threshold. After all, he had been feeling a bit better.

Jimmy died on Sunday, February 28, 2010, less than a week after being moved to hospice care. When he died, Ramona and Jessica were holding his hand. Ramona's parents were in the room. A nurse sang, maybe "Amazing Grace." Jimmy's friends, who had become more like brothers building wheelchair ramps together, found out about his death that morning. They were all in the Sunday morning service at Woodbine United Methodist Church. Billy says it was a "bittersweet" moment. On the one hand, one of his best friends had died. But on the other hand, he knew how his friend had suffered, and understood that the suffering was now over.

"It was tough," Billy says.

At his funeral on March 3, 2010, the "Angels in our Midst" spotlight on the wheelchair ramp ministry and Jimmy was shown. At his funeral, and at the two-hour visitation the night before, tons of people showed up to pay their respects. It was overwhelming.

"People just loved him," Jessica says.

Chapter 10: God has provided

They were some mighty big shoes to fill. Stan Holmes was taking over as the head of the wheelchair ramp ministry after Jimmy's death. He was not a handyman. He did not know about lumber, tools, and working with his hands. He never really built anything. He was intimidated when he first started volunteering. His volunteering had consisted of standing around a lot. He took his son to one ramp build and told him that if the experience was not fun, he would never ask him to come back. Well, it was not fun. Stan almost quit, until he noticed the handrails.

The completion of the handrails was the final piece to the ramp-building puzzle. He told himself that he would start working on those. He watched how they were done, and he slowly figured it out. From there, he became the "handrail guy," which he still is today. Stan jokes that he is the handrail guy because they are not a lot of fun and are difficult. Most volunteers want to lay the decking, pull the trigger on the nail gun. But those handrails kept him connected to the ministry. As he got more involved, he grew closer to Jimmy. He connected with Jimmy's mission.

"It was all about serving God," Stan says. "It was all about doing the right thing for God's people. He was the absolute picture-perfect picture of a Christian. He did it for the love of Jesus Christ and the love in his heart. That was it."

Stan understands the need to help others. His son, Matt, is autistic, his son's life through high school graduation chronicled in the book, "Matt's Journey: A Young Man's Journey Through Autism." The book follows Matt's life from his toddler days, to life in Korea and Arizona and Florida, to middle school and through high school. It is a story of fortitude and a relentless desire to find success against all odds.

Stan quickly learned just how much patience he was going to need to run the wheelchair ramp ministry, patience that he knew Jimmy had. How did Jimmy accrue all this information? How did he keep up with it all? Who helped him? How did he determine who would receive a wheelchair ramp? Why was that person chosen? How much lumber was needed? How many volunteers would commit to helping on a particular Saturday? Where would the money to buy the materials come from? Who would pick up the materials? Who would cook breakfast for the volunteers and order lunch? Perhaps most importantly, who would have the time to do all this, combined with everyday living and a full-time job? There were many questions to be answered.

God had always taken care of the wheelchair ramp ministry. There were many times when the money was not there in the church's budget to build the next ramp, and at the last hour, some anonymous donation came through.

"And every single time that has happened, miraculously, we got the money," Stan says.

Stan remembers an area manager at a Xerox store finding out about the ministry and coming to a ramp build with three or four co-workers. They had fun helping. Shortly after that build, the ministry began to run out of money. One night, Stan received an email from that store manager, asking when the next build was going to be. He told her that the ministry was on the verge of taking a break due to financial struggles. She sent back a one-line email response that read, "Would thirty-five hundred dollars help?" She handed him a check for that amount at the next build.

"That's just a perfect example of how God has provided for this ministry," Stan says. "We've really just been building ever since."

Another time, Stan stood in the pulpit at Woodbine United Methodist Church, telling churchgoers about the ministry's need for volunteers and donations. When Jimmy led the ministry, he never stood up front to speak. He was rather unassuming in those situations, choosing instead to sit near the back. He was an under-the-radar kind of guy, which made his success at leading the ministry that much more impressive. After speaking to the congregation, Stan stepped off the stage and was called over by an older woman with cerebral palsy, for whom the ministry had already built a ramp. She did not walk, and her words were hard to understand. Stan stood by her as she fiddled around in her purse. She pulled out a five-dollar bill and handed it to Stan, who knew she was one of the poorest people in the congregation. He instantly thought of Luke 21: 1-4, the verses about a poor widow putting two mites into the treasury as the rich put their gifts in. Jesus then said, "Truly I tell you, this poor widow has put in more than all the others. All these people gave their gifts out of their wealth; but she out of her poverty put in all she had to live on."

"That five dollars was a big deal to her," Stan says.

On the other end of the financial spectrum, a wealthy church member wrote Stan a check for one thousand dollars like it was nothing.

"I was just dumbstruck," he says.

He says that has happened so often that not one time has the group told anyone that it could not afford to build their ramp. The group has had to postpone due to bad weather, but never has it been a lack of money. More often than anything, the group has had to tell people their ramp cannot be built right away. The waiting list is just too long.

*****

IMPACT 100 Pensacola Bay Area, Inc. is an organization of women that is committed to improving nearby communities by providing grants to nonprofit organizations in Escambia and Santa Rosa counties. The group was started by four local women in 2003, and it has since become the largest IMPACT organization in the world. IMPACT recruits at least one hundred women who donate one thousand dollars each. The money is then pooled into grants worth at least one hundred thousand dollars each.

Before Jimmy passed away in 2010, he had applied for a grant through IMPACT 100. The wheelchair ramp ministry was not selected for a grant because it was not a true nonprofit organization at that time. It was solely a religious organization. There was a remedy for that.

"I can fix that," Stan said at the time.

Stan went through all the paperwork and created a 501c3 nonprofit organization. He fittingly named it Ray of Hope, after Jimmy. A year after Jimmy passed away, after not being selected for the grant, Stan applied for it again. He wrote a much better application with the help of Jessica, Jimmy's daughter. He remembers more than thirty nonprofit organizations applying. Those are tough odds. He figured the ramp ministry to be out of its league. But, as always, the

Lord provided for the wheelchair ramp ministry.

    Ray of Hope won the grant for the year 2011 in the family focus area, one of five grant winners. The impact was substantial. Ray of Hope earned a grant of more than one-hundred-seven-thousand dollars, which funded lumber, tools and a new truck, since the one the group had used had logged more than three-hundred-twenty-four-thousand miles. The money allowed volunteers to construct ninety-five wheelchair ramps for individuals previously confined to their homes. Stan says it took Ray of Hope thirteen or fourteen months to spend that money.

*****

    After Jimmy died, there was doubt about the wheelchair ramp ministry's future. Any person's intense passion is nearly impossible to replicate, but especially Jimmy's. He was the most persistent person. He would call people and ask for help, for resources. Most of the time, when a longtime leader of any group passes away or moves on to another position, that organization struggles. There is disorganization, rocky transitions. Sometimes, that organization fails.

Ramona worried that without Jimmy, the ministry would fizzle. Speaking about her husband from her new Birmingham home in 2016, she considers another thought. Sure, Jimmy's passion could not be matched, but his buddies had witnessed it. Seeing that passion, they would surely not let him down. Jimmy once had an old Dodge truck that Ramona's father gave to him. The passenger's side floorboard was rusted out. When a trailer had to be pulled, the truck simply got no power. It was on its last legs. To this day, Ramona does not know how, but the guys with the wheelchair ramp ministry pooled together some funds and bought him another Dodge truck, maybe two or three years old, big and tough-looking like the one Chuck Norris cut through the dust in "Walker, Texas Ranger."

Jimmy did not have somewhere to store his tools, so a diamond-plated toolbox was bolted behind the cab a few weeks after he received the truck. Jimmy came home from church one Wednesday night to find that gift.

"He was like a kid at Christmas over that toolbox, and we were amazed all over again at the generosity of those Woodbine guys," Ramona says.

He was so proud of that truck.

"That is how much they cared about him," Ramona says. "If they would buy him a pickup truck, surely they would keep building ramps."

Billy Pittman, one of Jimmy's best friends, was not sure if, or for how long, the ministry would continue. He knew that Stan had a grip on running it and keeping it going.

"If it is meant to go on, then God will find a way for it to go on," Billy says of his thinking at the time. "If not, it won't."

God found a way. Not only did the wheelchair ramp ministry continue, it flourished. There are many things in this world that need to keep going, services that people need to just get by, to survive. Jessica stops short of calling it a miracle that Ray of Hope continued under Stan's leadership, but she knows it is close.

"God is the only answer I have for that," she says.

Chapter 11: Angels again

Six years after the local ABC television news affiliate in Pensacola ran a segment about the wheelchair ramp ministry, just over a year after Jimmy's death, the "Angels in our Midst" segment came calling again. It was May 30, 2011.

The setting was a large white mobile home with forest-green shutters. Resting on a small wooden porch were two rocking chairs, a plastic white lawn chair and two big ceramic flower pots. The front yard was littered with long, thick pieces of wood, posthole diggers and other equipment. The Ray of Hope volunteers were hard at work.

The story is on a seven-year-old boy with cerebral palsy, born at twenty-four weeks old and weighing just one pound, seven ounces. Watching the video, it seems impossible that these young parents could have a seven-year-old. The boy stayed in the hospital for eight months before he came home. At seven years old, the boy weighed sixty-five pounds, and his parents were having to carry him in and out of the house. That daily labor was straining the parents' backs and knees. They needed help. The ramp that Ray of Hope built for the family was the two-hundred-ninety-sixth. In the video story, the reporter's voice states that the ministry was named Ray of Hope in honor of Jimmy, and that the group's members were still on his mission, lifting the burden of others. In the video story, Stan Holmes describes a wheelchair ramp constructed earlier in 2011. He states that the man had not left his home in six months. He was unable to go to the doctor, or anywhere, for that matter.

"That Saturday at about one o'clock in the afternoon, he hit the ground," Holmes says. "The Lord said, 'When you do these things for the least of mine, you do them unto me.' And that really is the Bible verse that we base this ministry on."

Mark Sopris, a Ray of Hope volunteer, says in the interview that they are called to help people in need. They are keeping Jimmy Ray's vision going.

"We're called to put our feet to the ground and go, so that's basically what we do," he says.

After the ramp is built for the boy, his mother says it is one more stress off everything they are going through. The boy's father estimates the ramp costing close to two thousand dollars, money that would have been hard, maybe impossible, to come by themselves. Everything these days seems so expensive.

"I was just really, really appreciative," the mother says. "So grateful that we could have somebody come help us. We really, really needed it."

The video story ends with a group of about ten volunteers praying over the family and the newly completed ramp. The boy sits in his wheelchair in the center of the ramp, his head bowed. The reporter's voice comes on again, saying, "Leaving a grateful family, they'll be off to bring another ray of hope in another little corner of their world."

The boy's father speaks the final five words of the nearly three-minute video. "Tell them thank you, son."

Part 2

Chapter 12: Cold-calling

Cold-calling strangers is not a strength of mine. It is actually quite nerve-racking. Selling insurance or some other product over the phone is the last type of job I would seek. I would most likely fail at it. I like to have already met someone before I call them on the phone. I like knowing that someone will pick up the phone because they recognize my number and are expecting my call. Put simply, I am a fan of organization and not of surprises. I am an unmitigated and unapologetic preparer.

For this book, I typed up my questions for Ray of Hope volunteers and wheelchair ramp recipients ahead of interviews, ordering the questions chronologically, so that my transcription of interviews flowed properly. That made writing each chapter a lot easier and quicker. I printed off dozens of copies, one for each person I would speak with. I scribbled names, which number recording it was and any other notes on these sheets. I kept a black notebook full of information for this book, complete with a lengthy list of wheelchair ramp recipients written in pencil on yellow notepad paper, scribbled down and mailed to me from Ed Lutes. I kept two lines blank under each name I had written out in a black notebook, one for their phone numbers, the other for notes about my call.

    I began making calls to wheelchair ramp recipients in late October 2016, after work and before a high school football game one Friday night, a defensive battle between Briarwood Christian School and Pleasant Grove High School in Birmingham. I interviewed a woman whose boyfriend was a recipient of a wheelchair ramp. The ramp was built leading into their mobile home in Milton, Florida. She was so thankful for the ramp and its impact, so pleased that a book chronicling the Ray of Hope organization was going to be published. Interviewing that lady produced a twenty-minute recording. She told me all about her boyfriend and his health issues, and the process for helping him in and out of the house before the wheelchair ramp was built. After several years of doing the job, a journalist can tell pretty quickly who is going to be a successful interview subject. This lady had that gift. Her words were detailed and thoughtful. She had a detailed answer for all of my questions.

Ten minutes later, I called the next person on the list, an older man who lived in Pensacola, Florida. His interview lasted just eight minutes and thirty-three seconds. His answers to my questions were unadorned and somewhat disturbing. I could hear a television show, which sure sounded like "Wheel of Fortune," blaring in the background. The man's answers to my questions consisted of few words, but he did mention the car wreck in the early 1980s that significantly injured him. Other than that, the interview was done, the man perhaps distracted by the game show's bonus round. But, when you are cold-calling folks you do not know for a book, any interview, any person who does not hang up on you, is a plus. I was two-for-two and encouraged. I had dreams of speaking to dozens upon dozens of people, maybe close to a hundred. After the 2016 holiday season, getting a hold of people became more difficult.

The first person I tried, a woman on Q Street in Pensacola, had a phone number that was no longer in service. The next phone number I dialed belonged to someone with a different name than what was on my list. Another woman answered one of my next calls and said that the person I was asking for was her daughter, but she must have thought I was scamming her, because she became defensive and chose to tell me that her daughter could not come to the phone. Perhaps I did not sell my idea quick enough. One number I dialed continuously rang, no one ever picking up, no voicemail or answering machine to stop the ringing. I had been told that one lady on the list may have passed away, and I imagined that to be true when I dialed the number under her name and was greeted again by the monotone voice: "We're sorry, you have reached a number that has been disconnected or is no longer in service. If you feel you have reached this recording in error, please check the number and try your call again." Many people never answered the phone, leaving me to mark a "N/A" off to the left of their names. I left voicemails for people who never called back and was unable to leave messages for those who had full voicemail inboxes. From a list of forty people, I made a total of sixty-four phone calls, attempting to call several people back a second and third time in hopes that they would answer. Out of the forty people, I interviewed fifteen. Twelve numbers were no longer in service or no longer belonged to the wheelchair ramp recipients who once owned them. I left voicemails and never heard back from eight people. Five numbers that I dialed continuously rang.

    But quite a few people did answer, and the following chapters are the results of those phone calls. There was the daughter who spoke of life before and after the wheelchair ramp built for her mother, who was having an electrocardiogram test at the hospital as we spoke. There was the woman who seemingly hung up on me on a Tuesday as I explained this book I was working on, only to have her call me back two days later and propagate her strong faith to me for twenty minutes. She apologized for hanging up on me, stating that she had been in a car accident the day I called. She was the most positive person I have ever spoken with over the phone.

    There was the elderly lady from Pensacola's Carriage Hills area, who had lost her husband not quite nine months before I called her. She sang

Ray of Hope's praises, and she sang, sang, sang. She told me that she would pray for God to allow me to finish this book, that it would be completed how I envisioned it from the get-go. She also said that she hoped God would keep her alive long enough to read it.

"I hope it has the effect on people I hope it has on them," she told me.

There were, of course, more moments just like that, poignant and inspiring. Each one humbled me in its own way, each story unique. These interviews compelled me just a little bit more to write this book to the best of my ability, to re-work that one sentence, to find that better adjective. The people who received these wheelchair ramps deserved that sort of effort from the author taking on this project. So did the Ray of Hope volunteers. So did Jimmy Ray, and his family.

Near the end of each interview that I conducted, I asked the man or woman about Jimmy Ray. I asked them that if he was still alive, still building wheelchair ramps, still changing lives because of what God led him to do, what would they say to him. I knew that it was a hypothetical question, but I had to ask. Some took a few moments to

gather their emotions and thoughts, knowing the name of the man who started all this. Some answered immediately. Some did not know what to say. But when they did respond, their answers were pretty much all the same.
    "I would tell him thank you."

Chapter 13: Dedicated and compassionate

Patsy grew up with Ramona, Jimmy's wife, on a road that wasn't paved until the two were teenagers. They were next-door neighbors and rode bicycles together.

When Ramona and Jimmy were married, they, for a time, attended the church in Milton, Florida, that Patsy's husband pastored.

"He was very faithful to come, to attend church," Patsy says of Jimmy, a man that she did not know all that well. "He was extremely faithful."

Patsy had a cousin whose mother died young due to multiple sclerosis. When that cousin was in her thirties, she discovered that she had the same disease, just like her mom.

Her cousin lived alone in a mobile home that required her to hang on to anything she could to get down the steps to her wheelchair. Inside the home, she had to lean on various things when she wasn't in her wheelchair. For a long time, the multiple sclerosis was severe. She had to give up her driver's license, leaving her to rely on neighbors for rides to the doctor and for groceries to be brought to her. Patsy often checked on her.

"She was having a hard time having any mobility of her own," she says.

Patsy, having known Ramona for so many years, was familiar with the Ray of Hope wheelchair ramp ministry. She put in a request for her cousin. Patsy's brother, who works in construction, supplied the materials for the project. Ray of Hope came on a Saturday and built an extra-long ramp so that the incline wasn't severe. The group even built a small slope from the mobile home down to a small porch so that she could get out even easier. It gave her mobility, and the ability to get to the yard and walk her little dog.

"It was a tremendous blessing to her," Patsy says. "It is definitely a needed ministry, and it was totally a blessing to her to have it. It was a wonderful thing for her to be able to have a little mobility of her own."

After three or four years using the ramp and living at the mobile home, the multiple sclerosis forced her to sell the home. She could not function alone anymore.

"It was a tremendous blessing for the three or four years she used it," Patsy says.

Patsy knows that her cousin would say that she's "extremely grateful" for the wheelchair ramp. Before she bought the mobile home, it had a ramp on its back side. The sellers thought that the ramp would keep the house from selling, so they removed it. As the multiple sclerosis worsened, she was desperate for some help. That is when Patsy enlisted the help of Ray of Hope.

Because Patsy and her husband have been in ministry all their lives, they have seen many missions and outreach initiatives. Ray of Hope is one she believes needs to continue.

"There is so much negativity, things that happen that are bad in the news, that it is great to hear a great story where people are actually helping each other," she says. "They're very dedicated and compassionate. And we need more of that."

Chapter 14: That ramp is a godsend

The motorcycle accident was bad. When he went down with the bike, its motor became intertwined with his left leg. It was gruesome. He had to have his left leg amputated from the knee down. He was just seventeen years old at the time.

After using an artificial prosthetic leg for years, the man began having pain in that leg. He wasn't getting enough blood circulation. He would walk on that prosthetic leg for five, maybe ten minutes, and have to go inside to lie down and rest. The man's girlfriend, who has been with him nearly fourteen years, tried to find a surgeon to amputate more of that leg, for increased blood flow. It was hard finding a surgeon. It was harder for the man to get in and out of the couple's Milton, Florida, mobile home. In the meantime, his girlfriend was told by a neighbor that Ray of Hope had built a wheelchair ramp for a relative in nearby Gulf Breeze. The neighbor got her the phone number, and she called. She was put on a waiting list.

The waiting list is long. The man remained on it for three years, until late summer 2016, when he found out that he was having another surgery. His girlfriend called Ray of Hope and told the group that he was having surgery in a week. She needed that ramp built as soon as possible. One of the Ray of Hope leaders called her on a Saturday morning, and said that the crew would be showing up that morning. The ramp was built before the afternoon hours. By that afternoon, the boyfriend was coming in and out of the mobile home on his motorized wheelchair.

"I am so happy with it," his girlfriend says. "He couldn't believe it. They did such a fantastic job. I couldn't believe it."

Now, the man can steer his motorized wheelchair down the ramp and into the yard, something he could not do before. The mobile home has four or five steps. He can sit in the yard with the couple's three small dogs. He can visit neighbors. He can get outside problem-free.

"That ramp, oh, it is a godsend," his girlfriend says. "It's a godsend. It really is."

Without that ramp, the girlfriend doesn't know what she would have done. Her boyfriend would have had to use a walker or learn to go up and down those stairs on crutches. He would have been scared to do either after surgery, she says. She would have had to find a way to lug his wheelchair in and out. Wheelchairs are heavy.

She says it again: "That ramp is such a godsend."

Now, she pays it forward. One day after the ramp was built, she was in the waiting room of a doctor's office, chatting with a woman who must have been in her eighties. The woman talked about how her husband needed a wheelchair ramp because of how difficult it had become for him to get in and out of their home. The girlfriend of the man who had just received a ramp told her about Ray of Hope and gave her the contact information. She keeps that information with her now, for moments such as this.

Chapter 15: They helped me a whole lot

The interview lasted only eight minutes and thirty-three seconds, and that brevity is the fault of us both. I called the Pensacola man on a Friday evening, before a high school football game I was covering for a local newspaper. I told him who I was and the project I was working on. I asked him if he would like to be a part of this book, to tell me his story. He told me that he was handicapped, having only one leg.

"That's about it," he told me.

I asked him if it would be all right if I asked him a few more questions. He said that was fine. I could hear the volume of a television in the background, and it sounded like a game show, likely "Wheel of Fortune," the show given away by the sound of that spinning wheel. His answers were blunt and shocking. And that is where the blame comes in. He could have turned the volume down and spoken more, and I, the interviewer, could have pressed him for more words. But the words were simply too astonishing. I was rendered speechless.

The man, Doug, had a wheelchair ramp built in July 2016. He lives in a mobile home in Pensacola, and it has steps. He can't climb them too well on crutches. He has just one leg, the missing one taken in an automobile accident in 1982. I asked him how the wreck transpired. Was he T-boned by a distracted driver at an intersection? How was the other driver? Did he run off a slick road into a ditch? Was he the driver or the passenger? He offers just once sentence.

"I was in the back floorboard, and my leg was in the trunk."

I was stunned. How was that even possible? Was he fibbing? Instead of probing any further, I just sat there in disbelief. What do you say to that?

He tells me that he got Woodbine United Methodist Church's phone number from the area Council on Aging. Ray of Hope soon came to Doug's home and built the wheelchair ramp. Being a veteran -- he spent one year, two months and ten days in the Navy -- Doug was moved up the waiting list. He says that nine men and two boys came to his home, set up equipment, and built the ramp in two-and-a-half hours.

"They were doing pretty good," he says.

Doug was finally opening up in our interview. He tells me that before the ramp, he used crutches to come up and down his front steps. After the ramp was built, he still used his crutches, but it is much easier now.

"Now it's fantastic," he says.

Doug lives off Social Security, and he would not have been able to afford a ramp on his own. For a while, he wondered how he would ever get it done.

"It meant a lot, because I didn't know what I was going to do," he says. "I'm supposed to have surgery on my one knee I have. If I had surgery and didn't have the ramp, I wouldn't have any way to get in and out on my wheelchair or scooter. I wouldn't know what to do."

Doug doesn't have to worry now. In fact, he tells people about what the Ray of Hope group did for him.

"They helped me a whole lot," he says.

Chapter 16: A blessing that can never be taken away

She spoke to me from the hallway of a northwest Florida hospital, where her eighty-seven-year-old mother was undergoing an electrocardiogram.

She didn't have to answer the phone call from a stranger in Birmingham, Alabama, but she did, pausing for only a few moments in a fifteen-minute conversation to hear an update from a nurse.

Ray of Hope built a wheelchair ramp at her home for her mother, who often stayed there. Her mother had back problems and fading eyesight. A wheelchair ramp was much-needed at her home. The front steps are steep.

"We couldn't get her up and down the steps," the daughter says. "It just took her all she could do. It just took everything out of her."

Fifteen to twenty Ray of Hope volunteers were able to build her a wheelchair ramp in one day. They came early in the morning with loads of lumber.

"They all worked together," the daughter says. "It was a combination of the younger generation, the middle, and the older generation. They came together and worked really, really well together. It didn't cost us anything. That was something in itself. We just didn't have the funds."

The older volunteers taught the youngsters how to run the tools, how to swing hammers. The daughter offered to make the group lunch, but Woodbine United Methodist Church in Pace brought some.

"Each one of them had a different job, and each one knew exactly what it was," she says.

The group prayed before building the ramp and prayed over the completed project.

"It's been a godsend," the daughter says. "My mother has a wheelchair, too, but she tries to stay out of it as much as possible, but she also has a little walker, too. I thought it was great. It was a blessing, just a blessing that can never be taken away. It showed us how much people really do care, and how they can come together when they're in the right place at the right time."

The daughter pondered the idea of Ray of Hope not building her a wheelchair ramp, not existing as a nonprofit organization. She laughed.

"I'd probably have to go stay with her because she has an old (ramp) at her home, but it's fixing to have to be replaced," she says. "Her ramp is not nearly as well built as this one. And, of course, it wasn't built with the love that this one was built with. So caring. I think it's a good thing that they're doing, and I think there needs to be more of it."

I told this woman about Jimmy Ray, the man who started the Ray of Hope wheelchair ramp ministry at Woodbine United Methodist Church. I told her about his concern for others in need, his passion for getting wheelchair ramps built for the elderly and homebound.

"I would just thank him from the bottom of my heart and, you know, (I'd tell him) that God put him here for that reason, a sole purpose," she says. "For somebody else to pick it up and carry it on is just godsent. We need more people like him."

She told me that her brother and sister-in-law were members at Woodbine, and that she and her mother were about to join as well. I asked if they were joining, in part, due to the Ray of Hope group.

"That's a large factor," she says. "It's like family. You know, you just can't firmly depend on anybody but family. They got out there and did what they had to do and didn't ask us for anything. We had prayer and everything after it was built, and I'll never forget about that. They blessed all the people who might have to use (the ramp). I'll never forget about that."

Chapter 17: They build with heart

She was eager to talk about her family's experience with Ray of Hope, but she had one stipulation.

"If I cry, you'll just have to excuse me," she told me.

Yes, ma'am.

The wheelchair ramp was built in January 2015, and it was for her twenty-six-year-old son. He was born with a spinal deformity, which did not manifest itself until his teenage years. He was injured in a high school football game as a member of the Pace High School team, ending his career. He stayed on as the team manager.

He was in the student government at Pace High School. At Florida State University, he was elected captain of the paintball team and was a member of a fraternity, in which he served as risk manager. He loved football, hunting, and things from bygone eras. He was quick-witted and a historical trivia master. His family didn't need Google with him around.

"He was very independent and very smart," his mother says. "He was in the gifted program and got scholarships from all sorts of colleges. But to lose your independence and to have to be dependent on your parents, the ramp helped him gain some sort of independence. He didn't have to rely on us to transfer him from the car to the house."

Her son had developed an infection on his spine that worsened over time. It affected his T6-T12 vertebrae, and while in rehabilitation, the family was told that he needed a wheelchair ramp for the wheelchair he was going home in. His mother was made aware of this on a Wednesday, and he was going home that Friday.

"Well, I panicked because we have steps up to our front door," the mother says. "He was twenty-six and too big for me or my husband to carry from the car to the house."

The mother's cousin told her that Ray of Hope built wheelchair ramps for those in need.

"I don't know (what we would have done without Ray of Hope)," she says. "I honestly do not know. I was in a little bit of a terror not knowing what to do, but I was so happy when my cousin said to try their number. It was really a true blessing. I don't know what we would have done."

She was put in touch with Stan Holmes, whose son went to school with her son. She remembered that when her son was in third grade, Stan's son was being picked on, so her son took up for him. She remembered Stan's wife calling to tell her about it.

"It meant a lot to her," she said.

Stan was going out of town that Friday, so he came that Wednesday and began building the ramp. He finished the twenty-foot ramp Thursday. By himself.

"That's very special to us," she says. "I just told everybody about it. I tell everybody how wonderful it is because of that. It was ready when (my son) got out of the hospital on Friday afternoon. It was ready, completed."

She says that during her son's rehabilitation, one of the physical therapists had volunteered with Ray of Hope in the past.

"The people on there, who donate their time to do that, are really amazing," she says. "I think it's a wonderful ministry. If I could give them all the money I had, I would do it. I think they're just wonderful."

Her son got better over time, graduating from a wheelchair to a walker. The ramp stayed in place because he still could not maneuver the front steps. It gave him a little bit of independence back.

"That was just a blessing to us," she says.

Her son died in May 2016 from health complications. His obituary stated that he had a special relationship with his mother, that he would call her every day on his way home from work to talk about the day's events.

I told her that Ray of Hope had built more than five hundred wheelchair ramps, that more than five hundred families had been blessed by this group. She was not shocked.

"That doesn't surprise me because I think they build with heart, but that's amazing," she says. "It's always going to be close to my heart. For me, it was my child. I will never forget it."

Oh, and she never cried. I'm not sure how.

Chapter 18: Like a kid going down a hill

The woman's husband had become paralyzed on his left side after a stroke. He was partially blind. A portion of his brain was removed during surgery.

The woman needed a wheelchair ramp to help her husband in and out of their home in Milton, Florida. They had just one front step, but she often had to give her husband's wheelchair an "oomph" to get him over it and inside. It would shake him in his chair.

In June 2016, she got something that she had wished for.

The woman's mother-in-law was affiliated with Woodbine United Methodist Church in Pace, Florida, where Jimmy Ray started the Ray of Hope wheelchair ramp ministry. That's how she found out about the group.

Before the woman brought her husband home from rehabilitation, the Ray of Hope group had built and installed a wheelchair ramp at their home. When they arrived home, she was floored. She knew Ray of Hope was coming sometime, but she hadn't known the exact day. What a surprise.

"Wow, this is wonderful," the woman recalls thinking that day.

The woman's husband has since passed away, but that wheelchair ramp provided some light in a dark time in their lives. She was able to help him in and out of the house without jarring him or causing herself pain. He enjoyed going up and down the ramp.

"He would get to the point where if I opened the front door, he'd go down the ramp and out into the yard on the wheelchair like a kid going down a hill," the woman says. "He did (have fun). It made it much easier on me, and I know he appreciated that. It was such a blessing and such a help in a really crucial time of need."

The ramp made it easy to bring the wheelchair in and out of the house. Wheelchairs are heavy and awkward to lift.

"It just made all the difference in the world," she says. "It made it so much easier, and I hated jarring him. He had enough..." She trails off.

The wheelchair ramp has since been taken off her front porch, but she still has it. She hopes that Ray of Hope can use it for someone else in need. She knows the organization has built more than five hundred wheelchair ramps.

"It doesn't surprise me because they were so passionate about it," she says. "It touches me because they performed a service that is so needed. Until you encounter being handicapped or having a handicapped person close to you, you have no idea the inconvenience that it is in different places. And if they're able to make it a little more helpful … they just have no idea how much of a blessing that was."

The woman says that people near and far need to know about the Ray of Hope group and what it does for others. So much attention these days is paid to talking heads on twenty-four-hour political news channels, celebrities whining on social media, and unrest across the globe.

"Because I think people need to know there are good people out there, and there are helpful people doing what God intended for them to do to help others," the woman says. "There are not enough people like that out there. It's just sad."

She is asked if she hopes Ray of Hope can get to the magical number of one thousand wheelchair ramps built for people in need. She takes it even further.

"Oh, absolutely, or more," she says. "Two, three, five thousand."

Chapter 19: By the grace of God

It was like talking on the phone with your grandmother.

She was sweet, caring, and you knew that she'd bake you an apple pie if you just asked nicely. Her voice was velvety soft, and she was full of emotion. The softness almost turned to a squeal when she was recalling a pleasant memory. It faded into the background when she let herself feel pain again.

This woman from Pensacola, Florida, had a wheelchair ramp built by Ray of Hope in early 2015. It was for her son, a fifty-eight-year-old man on dialysis for liver cancer. He had been sick for a couple years, but the last part of his sickness was finding out about the liver cancer.

"It was ... it was just kind of devastating," his mother says. "After he finally went through radiation and chemotherapy and stuff, they said that it was gone but yet still his surgeon wanted to operate I guess to get it all out or whatever."

Because of his condition, he needed a wheelchair ramp to get in and out of the house. He had been on the

Ray of Hope waiting list for two or three months, maybe more, and one day the group showed up. The mother says they were nice and professional people who built a "magnificent ramp."

"He was in great need before the ramp was built," she says. "He suffered a lot with his illness. Nevertheless, he was very appreciative, and so was I."

The day the ramp was built was an exciting time for mother and son.

"I was very blessed, and he was, too, because I had been waiting on the list and that day was like a surprise," she says. "I was excited. My son was, too. I was very happy. It was a good feeling because I was tired of trying to get him out of the house without a wheelchair or walker, you know?"

The ramp totally changed their lives.

"Because, you know, then I didn't have a problem," she says. "I could wheel him out of the house. He could sit in the car, and then I could put the wheelchair in the back of the car. Then he was on dialysis and they had to pick him up sometimes if I wasn't able to bring him. It was just an awesome time for me, I know. It helped me a lot."

That old-school toughness shined through when I asked her what she would have done had the ramp never been constructed.

"I would have done what I could, you know?" she says. "I probably would have had to pay somebody to help me get him in and out of the house in that wheelchair. That would have been the other thing I had to do. I was just kind of waiting. It's just by the grace of God that he didn't get worse before they got out to build it, so we could maintain (what we were doing)."

But a wheelchair ramp can only do so much. Two weeks after her son's surgery, he had a heart attack. A heart attack so soon after a major surgery complicates progress. Her son was unable to eat. When he did eat, he could not keep the food down.

"That was really bad," she says, and her voice fades.

Her son was able to use the ramp for several months before he died in September 2015.

"Oh, yes," she says, when I ask if he was happy with the ramp. "I think so, and I don't know for sure because I try not to think about it a whole lot. Anyway,

I know it was a good thing as far as I'm concerned."

I can tell the conversation is slipping away. The pain is taking over. I transition.

"The man who started Ray of Hope was my father-in-law," I say. "If he was still here, what would you say to him?"

"I would give him a big hug and a kiss and just thank him," she answers. "There really probably wouldn't be too many words I could say other than 'Thank you' and 'I appreciate you.' I'm so glad he was a lover of people. He really was."

We talk about her life since her son's passing. We talk about a society obsessed with political and celebrity scandals, about how inconceivable it is that many men don't hold doors open for women anymore. Always in a hurry. I ask her if that makes the Ray of Hope group, given its heart for others, even more impressive.

"Oh, it's godsent," she says, and that pep in her voice is back. "Because in today's time people don't believe in helping people for nothing. They're going to charge you a whole lot of money for it. So, I think they're just godsent and they're doing this from their heart. These people got much love in their hearts for their fellow man. It's just great."

She says that she is grateful for people with love in their hearts and help others.

"That's what I try to do right now," she tells me. "I try to help anyone I can in any way I can. I try to practice being a missionary. I can at least tell somebody about God and about Jesus Christ and do whatever I can to help them. If I can take them somewhere or fix them a meal or something like that, I'll do that."

She tells me that the group reminds her of her grandparents, who raised her on a farm in Atmore, Alabama. She knew what it looked like for people to help others back then. Her grandparents would take in people coming from other cities looking for work. They would feed them and give them work until they moved on.

"So, Ray of Hope is sort of close to your heart because of everything you've seen in your life, good and bad?" I ask.

"Truly, sir," she says. "Truly."

Chapter 20: Led to help

The woman was ninety-one years old, and she still worked six days per week.

Do you work six days per week? I know I try my hardest not to.

She spent her time working with children with various disabilities, and while moving furniture one day, she fell. The fall hurt her bad enough that she had to move from her east Pensacola, Florida, home, a one-hundred-sixteen-year-old house built atop a steep hill, to her daughter's home.

"There was no way to get her in and out of the house," the daughter says.

She was in a wheelchair and at her daughter's house for six months. But when you are ninety-one years old, or comfortable in your own routines at any age, you want to be home, sleeping in your own bed, opening the correct cabinet for a coffee cup.

"My momma wanted to go home," the daughter says. "She had been here six months and she was ninety-one years old and she wanted to go home, and she got to go home because of them. She would not have been able to, had they not come and given us that blessing."

The "they" she refers to are the four or five volunteers from Ray of Hope who came one day around Christmas 2015 to build a wheelchair ramp so that the woman could move back home. Her daughter paid for the lumber and materials so that the project could be completed as soon as possible. Otherwise, there would have been a three-month wait.

"We had the ramp within three weeks," she says. "I thought that was wonderful. It truly is a wonderful ministry. I mean, we just felt so blessed when they helped us."

The daughter helps her mother with her daily errands, while the elderly woman's son stays with her to help her at home. Despite the family German Shepherd "christening the ramp" when it was completed, the daughter says that Ray of Hope was a wonderful blessing to her family.

"We tell people about it often because it really was a blessing to us," she says. "My brother doesn't know a nail from a hammer and my husband drove coast to coast, and I just lost him this past six months ago to cancer. We didn't have anybody to do it. Even our handyman could not do it."

Had Ray of Hope not existed, the elderly mother would have likely stayed with her daughter longer so that the family could find someone who could build a wheelchair ramp.

"I just really am in awe of people who, in this world, in this day in age when there is so much going on, people who are willing to take the time to help somebody in need," she says. "It just warms my heart. It's a wonderful thing. We don't hear about that. We hear about all this mess that's going on."

I tell her that it was my father-in-law who started the Ray of Hope group. I ask her, like I have asked so many, what she would say to him if he were still here, still measuring slopes for ramps and pounding nails into wood.

"I'd feel very indebted to him," she says.

She tells me that her mother was featured on a local television feature in Pensacola called "Angels in our Midst," about people doing positive things in their communities. She says that Ray of Hope, and Jimmy, would be great candidates for the show. I respond by telling her that both have been featured. This does not surprise her.

"I can't say anything bad about them," she says. "I think they just feel led to help people and to give back to the community. I think that God has just given them a talent that they're willing to share, and that's amazing."

She does say, however, that she wishes more people knew about Ray of Hope. She doesn't want to overload the group with requests, but she knows that there is a need. More than five hundred ramps built in the northwest Florida area proves that.

"I think that if people do something to give back, if they knew more about this ministry, they would be willing to donate," she says. "I don't think people are aware of it."

She says that every year, her family chooses some charity to donate to, some cause to support. Years ago, the family had a negative experience with one. They gave, but the recipient seemed ungrateful. The family donates to two or three different charities now rotationally. Ray of Hope is one of them. The family treats it like tithing.

"I feel like I can see and feel the help that it gives to other people," the daughter says.

Chapter 21: Good ol' country stuff

It was tough to decipher his words. Sure, they slurred because of his mumbling, but it was more than that.

I could hear dogs barking in the background. There were birds chirping. At one point during our twenty-minute conversation, a train blared its horn as it rolled down the tracks.

The wheelchair ramp was built for him around the time the calendar switched over to 2016. He doesn't remember how Ray of Hope found out about him, or how he found out about it. But somehow, they connected. There was a four-month waiting list, he was told.

In September 2014, the man had his right leg amputated above the knee. About a year later, doctors took the toes from his left foot. One doctor told him the reason for the amputations was cigarettes, while another said the cause was gangrene. The man guesses that the cigarettes caused the gangrene.

"Cigarettes do a lot of damage, whether people know it or not," he tells me.

Because of the two surgeries, the man asked his doctor for a remote-control scooter. Once he got it, he wondered how he was going to get in and out of his northwest Florida home. He has two steps he must navigate, and he had been using a walker. He had to be careful hopping up and down them.

Ray of Hope showed up on a Saturday afternoon and relieved the man of this struggle. He came out on his porch to watch the progress.

"With the ramp I don't have to worry about that (anymore)," he says. "I have the scooter and I just ride up. Tremendous."

He pauses and repeats himself. "Tremendous."

I tell him Ray of Hope has constructed more than five hundred ramps, and he is not shocked in the least. He says that he does wonder, "How could they have?" He answers his own question.

"Passion," he says. "Oh, man. Yeah, passion."

I then tell him that it was my father-in-law who started the wheelchair ramp ministry. I ask him if Jimmy was still alive, what would he say to him.

"Oh, man" he says twice after about ten seconds. It's obvious a heartstring has been tugged. He quips that he would get down on his one remaining knee and break down in tears. We both laugh.

"I would praise him so much," he says.

Without the wheelchair ramp, he would still be using that walker, trying his best not to fall down. He tells me that the day before we spoke, he got a prosthetic right leg. He says he can walk now, and that he is seeing the benefits already.

"I'm loving this," he says.

I ask him if there is anything else he wants to add for his chapter in the book, anything I failed to ask. He says that he lives out in the country, that he loves the outdoors. He often fished and hunted before he had his leg surgeries.

"Good ol' country stuff," he says.

After his right leg was taken, he mostly stayed in his house because he had to. He went as far as his porch, the one on which he sat while the Ray of Hope volunteers built his ramp. The great outdoors were at his fingertips.

Now, he can go to Wal-Mart by himself. He hasn't been fishing or hunting again yet, but that time is quickly approaching. He'll sit in a lawn chair and reel in a striped bass in the spring or drop an eight-point buck in the fall. For now, he just goes out into his yard on his scooter or on his prosthetic leg and appreciates what he can see and smell. He admires the flowers in his yard.

He says that Ray of Hope has had a tremendous impact on a lot of people, including himself. He tells me that he wants to read this book because he wants to see how other people feel about their wheelchair ramps, how Ray of Hope helped them out.

"I'm so glad they came over," he says, and I can now tell that all that background noise is because he must be on his porch or out in the yard.

He is appreciating as we speak.
"I'm so glad."

Chapter 22: I try to pray every day

I had written off this interview as a possibility.

When I called, she seemed angry and listened just long enough to hear my pitch about an interview for this book. She then hung up.

I moved on to others and tried to forget that I called. Two days later, she called me back. The day I called, she had been in a car accident and was out of sorts. Who wouldn't be?

She again seemed somewhat skeptical, but after a touch of convincing, she agreed to talk for the book.

"I would love to do it," she told me.

I don't remember the first question I asked her, but I made sure to note the words she responded with, about allowing God to do what He needs to do with her in this world.

"I have so much faith in God," she says. "He's the only one I trust my life with."

Ray of Hope had built her a wheelchair ramp a few months before we spoke. Her brother had a stroke in

October 2015 and was put on dialysis, and the ramp was for him. She was on dialysis, too. The timing was hard to decipher. She says that at the time, she called on God, while her brother was turning his back to God. He was giving up.

Once her brother came home from the hospital, an unclear incident occurred that forced her to call the police and have him put in jail. She can't live with him again due to the incident. She told me that she would help him find a place to stay once he leaves jail. If all goes well, she may consider allowing him to come back to her house.

She said she found out about Ray of Hope because the group had built a wheelchair ramp at her neighbor's house. She stopped by and asked who they were. Not long after, Ray of Hope was building a ramp at her house. The noise of hammers colliding with lumber woke her up one Saturday morning.

"To me, it was a blessing," she says. "I don't care if they did one foot. It would still be a blessing."

She didn't have to buy one scrap of material. Ray of Hope did it all, even the praying over the ramp when it was completed. She liked that a young man was there to help and was being taught how to use the various tools. She would like to see more of that, to help keep kids off the streets, away from drugs and trouble.

"It was just such a blessing to see that, because most people don't get that," she says.

She said that when she was growing up, kids were always outside, riding bicycles, and playing. There was encouragement from many relatives, neighbors, and friends. Now, the streets during the daylight are mostly quiet.

"Everybody is in their own world," she says. "Life has changed so much in so many ways for so many people."

While her brother lived with her, he would use a walker and try to get up and down the steps by himself. Staggering and falling on her four steps was a problem, even with help from her and neighbors. With the ramp, he could do it all on his own.

"It was a big help to me, and I thank God for it," she says. "It was a blessing."

The ramp was needed by her brother and her. They both had health struggles, but she is modest and doesn't talk much about herself. I asked her what she would have done without the ramp, and she started crying.

"Continue praying to God and hoping that He would bless me," she says. "I pray every day. I try to pray every day. I don't care if I just say, 'Thank you, Jesus.' I try to pray every day."

She made sure to mention to me that she was toying with the idea of writing a book about her life experiences and faith. She will need a computer to get it done, she told me. I told her that I thought it was a great idea and to have a great day.

"You, too, and be blessed," she said.

Yes, ma'am. And your brother, too.

Chapter 23: Not a dime

Catherine's wheelchair ramp was rotting, so she found herself in a tough spot.

She wondered what she would do, and who would help her. A friend of hers had a new wheelchair ramp, a nice one that Ray of Hope built for her. Her friend gave Catherine, in her early eighties at the time, the group's phone number.

Volunteers measured to determine the ramp's length, and not long after, Catherine had a new ramp. She was diabetic and didn't get around easily without her small walker, which she affectionately called her "four-wheeler." She watched Ray of Hope build her new ramp, from the first plank of wood to the final nail.

"They were just wonderful," she says.

After her new ramp was completed, the Ray of Hope group, as it always does, prayed over it, and with its recipient. A prayer was said for her health. Catherine was appreciative.

"I loved that, because I try to go to church when I can," she says. "I'm not able to go like I used to. I just thank them, and I thank the Lord for making a way for them for us that need it."

Her diabetes keeps her away from church sometimes, but she tries to go when she feels up to it. Her friends take her and bring her back home. She said her sugar levels are just about straightened out.

"I thank the Lord for that," she says.

I asked Catherine about how much she leans on her faith, how much it pains her to not be able to go to church when she wants to attend. The question made her think about how things used to be, and how they are now.

"As a people, we don't talk to each other anymore," she says. "We don't do that. We're supposed to love each other, and most of the time now, I don't care what kind of shape you're in, if you need something done real fast, you're going to have to dish out the money. I didn't have no money, I didn't have one dime when they came. I was glad, and I thank them for doing that for me. I always think about it, how they came and were so professional and everything, making sure that it was right and all."

Without Ray of Hope, Catherine would have had to find somebody else to build a ramp for her, and she likely would have had to come up with some money. Thankfully, she didn't have to. She appreciates her friend for passing along the Ray of Hope contact information, and the group for being so selfless.

"I love to see people help other people," Catherine says. "But it seems to me, and I've seen it in churches, too, the person you help is the person that doesn't really need help. Your friend or something like that. The Lord wants us to help the one that really needs our help, and there are a lot of folks out there like that. They need help. It might not be anything but handing them a drink of water. We don't visit each other like we used to years back when I was growing up either. Sit and talk with them for just a little while. You'd be surprised how much better they would feel when you leave them. And I always think about that. If there is anybody I can help, I will, if I can help them."

It doesn't surprise Catherine that Ray of Hope has helped more than five hundred people in need of wheelchair ramps. She has seen the need across northwest Florida.

"That many people need them. No, it doesn't shock me because I see so many people, older people, trying to get around, trying to get ways to the grocery store and get their medicine and all like that," she says. "Some of them don't have nobody help them out (of their house). They're trying to get out the best way they can. But I'm glad it's happening (all the ramps). I hope it will increase."

Me, too, Catherine. She says she sees a group such as Ray of Hope as the Lord's work being carried out.

"People are living longer today," she says. "You're going to get sick. You're going to need somebody's help. I'm glad to know there's somebody out there that can get past themselves and what they've got and help these other people."

Chapter 24: A dream come true

Most of the volunteers came on motorcycles, but the rumble of Harley Davidsons didn't wake up Eleanor. She was already wide awake and waiting.

Eleanor says people give motorcycle riders a bad name.

"That's just not fair," she says. "You've got to know who you're dealing with."

Eleanor says those men on motorcycles were godsent because they entered her life in a time of need in 2016. Her husband had battled Parkinson's disease for seven years, and his health was worsening. Hospice was called in that February so that he could be at home.

"I just can't say enough about these guys," Eleanor says. "They are godsent."

It had taken Eleanor a long time to get in touch with Ray of Hope, so a friend built a temporary wheelchair ramp out of plywood for her husband in the meantime. It didn't have handrails, and had he gathered any speed in his wheelchair, the ramp's flimsiness would have caused him to tip over.

When Ray of Hope came to her house, the volunteers built a long wheelchair ramp that angled toward the driveway, to get to the car easier. They even built a small ramp at the back door. I told Eleanor that it was amazing what the Ray of Hope group has done.

"It's a miracle," she says. "It was just a dream come true. God worked it out, and I just can't tell you, I don't know how to tell you how something like that is laid in your hands. What a wonderful group. I paid not one penny for this ramp. Somebody donated all the equipment, all of the materials for it. I can't tell you what it meant to us."

Eleanor thought building such a large wheelchair ramp would take at least a couple days. After all, the volunteers had to dig up her chain link fence before they even began hammering nails. Ray of Hope was finished just after lunch.

"Just amazing," she says.

She made the volunteers lunch as a surprise thank you, a spread consisting of ham, potato salad, sandwiches, and chips.

"That made me feel so great," she says. "I could give them a teeny, teeny portion of what they had done for us. They're just wonderful, wonderful people."

Her husband's health worsened significantly in March and April of 2016. The couple had to move their bedroom to the downstairs of their split-level home. They had the garage converted into a big living room with a half bathroom. Her husband died on April 27, 2016. He didn't get to take advantage of the wheelchair ramp much, though he was proud of it. It was built big enough that he could use it as a small porch, and he was able to sit outside once or twice and just look around.

"If you could just see what these people did for us, I can't praise them enough, I can't praise God enough for letting all this come through because they did such a wonderful job on this ramp," Eleanor says. "It was just working with people like that ... I will never forget them. I will never stop singing their praises because they helped us out in such a time of need. It's just amazing. I just can't tell you the blessing that they provided us."

I told Eleanor that Jimmy Ray started the Ray of Hope ministry, and that he was my father-in-law. I asked her what her thoughts were on someone starting an organization whose mission is simply to help others and expects nothing in return. She says that he had to be a man of God to help the less fortunate, the people with not a lot of money.

"He had to be a man of God to help people like us," she says. "(Money) just didn't matter. That didn't matter at all. All they were interested in was getting (the ramp built). I just can't praise them enough in the name of the Lord, because they were all Christian men. We prayed before, and we prayed when it was finished. It was just amazing. Amazing. I am so thankful that the Lord had come into my life in a time when I needed Him so bad."

Eleanor reiterates that because of how quickly her husband's health deteriorated, he didn't get to use the wheelchair ramp much. She mentioned, however, that she will be able to use it, to help her get in and out of the house easier when she needs to run errands.

"I know it's going to be a blessing for me," she says. "I really can't put into words how it affected my life. But the Christianity of these men was so heartwarming and so touching."

She says that the huge number of wheelchair ramps that have been built is "truly a work of the Lord" and that it "wakes up a lot of people that could do something."

"There just aren't enough words to be able to tell what I felt like they did for us," Eleanor says. "I just know the thrill and joy they had, and the time they took from their lives to do this. They seemed like they got so much joy out of doing this."

Chapter 25: I'll call them angels

The ramp was for her mother, who had had a stroke. She was in her nineties and was moving in with her daughter.

The daughter bought the materials for the project, and Ray of Hope came quickly. She worried about dealing with individuals as opposed to a national company with some sort of recourse, but Ray of Hope was "very, very professional," she says.

"They were in and out so fast," she says. "It was like the elves had been sent. Not elves. I'll call them angels."

Her mother uses the ramp for exercise, in addition to innocently spying on neighborhood happenings. She walks up and down it a few times per day.

"It works for her," her daughter says. "It made a tremendous difference. It's therapeutic for her."

She never imagined that her mother would have a stroke and move in with her. Before the ramp was built, her mother went on and on about wanting to go outside, but the steps were too high. The daughter had seen wheelchair ramps all over her Pensacola, Florida, neighborhood, so it didn't shock her that Ray of Hope has constructed more than five hundred of them.

"I just thought it was a wonderful thing for people to have if they needed them," she says. "It serves a very, very good purpose. It's real accessible to my car. She can go down the ramp to the car."

I ask this woman the deeper meaning of all this, of strangers building wheelchair ramps for other strangers. She takes off.

"I'm old school," she says. "When I was growing up you practically had no outreach, especially for black people. That's really comforting to know that we're just growing in diversity and growing in love and unity in providing services for anybody and everybody."

She tells me that when she was growing up, there was no true door-to-door help, especially from small churches, which tended to take care of their own. She is glad that a group like Ray of Hope, born from Jimmy's vision at Woodbine United Methodist Church, exists. She blends some scripture from the books of Matthew and John to illustrate her point.

"They're following the mission of Jesus," she says. "Go ye therefore and teach all nations. First, demonstrate the love of the Lord, demonstrate the love of Jesus. Love each other as I have loved you."

The daughter says the Ray of Hope volunteers had children with them, which impressed her.

"That's what missionaries are supposed to do," she says. "The Bible says to train up a child while he is young. It's always good to see Christians put their money where their mouth is. Don't just come to me and say you're a follower of Christ and, yet, you can't follow through. You've got to walk the walk, baby."

The daughter hopes that Ray of Hope keeps doing what it is doing, and her reasoning is more scientific than inspirational. People are living longer these days, she says, and babies are not as often dying prematurely. People with special needs are living longer, and Ray of Hope is enhancing their independence.

"Nobody wants to be dependent on anybody," she says. "People will hold onto their independence as long as they can, especially the elderly and children. Those two groups want to do it for themselves. Even if they fall down, they get back up."

You can't argue with that. She continues.

"We need more love, that's for sure," she says. "We need more Jesus in our hearts. I know that."

I tell her that Ray of Hope sure appears to be living this out.

"Well, that's the great commandment," she says. "We're supposed to do that. We're charged to do that. If we're not doing that, then we can't say we're followers of Christ. We want to be Christlike. We want to be just like Jesus -- walk the way he walked, talk the way he talked. God ain't sleeping. People don't have awareness that God is aware."

The conversation, which started out slow, has become a full-on sermon, and I'm just sitting in a creaky pew, nodding my head. She tells me that her daughter relocated to Fort Lauderdale, Florida, and was unsettled, unable to find a church. She gets in trouble with her mom if she doesn't find a church, the woman jokes to me.

"It's a good feeling to know that you brought your child up in the way of the Lord," she says. "Talking about the Lord, we could stay on the phone all night."

I believe it and tell her as much. An interview that at first seemed as if it would last maybe ten minutes has gone on for more than twenty. I ask if there is anything else she wants to add. She says that she referred one of the Ray of Hope leaders to her mother's beautician, since she thought so highly of the work the group did for her mother.

"I think what they're doing is wonderful," she says. "And we do need more people out there who can address the needs of those people who have whatever impediments they have."

I can tell she is thinking for a way to wrap this all up, to tie a bow on the gift of the last twenty minutes she has given me, and she tells me that every time she sees a wheelchair ramp now, she wonders if it was that Ray of Hope group that built it.

I tell her that as many as the group has built, more than five hundred, it very well could be.

Chapter 26: Away we go

The wheelchair ramp was for her husband, but he died before he really had the chance to use it.

He spent his remaining time on this earth in a rehabilitation and long-term care facility in Milton, Florida, and his wife, Pat, visited all the time. That constant going back and forth broke her body down.

"It just seems after he passed, my body gave up," Pat says. "I was just running on sparks."

Pat, who is eighty-three, has had multiple back surgeries in her life. One kept her for more than two months in the same rehabilitation facility where her husband died. She says it was difficult to pass the room where her husband passed away. She never wanted to see that room again.

"But there I was, for two and a half months, getting strong enough to use my own walker," she says.

She also "got handy" with using a wheelchair. She liked to make it go fast. When she goes outside, it is in a wheelchair. The ramp that was built by

Ray of Hope for her husband has benefited her.

"I don't know what we would have done without that ramp," she says. "I'll never forget it. I tell everybody."

The wheelchair ramp is massive. Pat's house sits five feet above ground, which means that length of slope required a lot of lumber. She remembers waking up one Saturday morning to a yard covered in pickup trucks and Ray of Hope volunteers, none of whom she knew. She cooked hamburgers for them all that afternoon. She never expected a gift like this, something by chance from strangers.

"And all of a sudden, there it was, right when we needed it the most," she says.

Pat found out about Ray of Hope from her doctor. She then called to request the ramp be built. She bought the materials, and Ray of Hope constructed the ramp in one day.

"I thought, 'Holy mackerel,'" she says of Ray of Hope's quick work. "Without it, oh, my goodness. I don't know what would have happened to me. I wouldn't be able to go to the doctors and stuff. They'd have to manually carry me. It's a godsend."

She thinks on it for a moment. Her house is five feet above the ground, so there are large steps. She is unable to walk up and down those. She says without the wheelchair ramp, she would be in deep trouble. She laughs.

"We'd have deep trouble trying to get me down to a car or anything," Pat says. "Now they just stick me in a wheelchair, and away we go."

Pat calls the wheelchair ramp her "God gift."

"People don't realize, if you just open up and tell somebody what you need, then sometimes you get help from a stranger," she says.

I ask Pat if there is anything else she wants to say, or if I have left anything out.

"All I can do is just to pray for the people coming up that need a ramp to be able to get in touch, that somebody will touch them, and be able to be connected, just like I did," she says. "If you're brave enough to call out to what you really need, maybe some ear will hear it."

Chapter 27: Everybody helped everybody

I have recorded and transcribed thousands of interviews. I have heard so many different things. I have heard football coaches and linebackers talk about defining stops on third down in the fourth quarter. I have heard city councilmen filibuster about tight budgets and important elections. I have spoken to a teenager who had beaten cancer twice, but I didn't get to interview him after his third bout. I have talked with a woman who drove more than one hundred people home in a snowstorm, and another woman who lost her wedding ring in a tornado. I have recorded interviews with school principals about inspiring teachers, lawmen about hardened criminals, and rich celebrities about themselves.

I could go on and on, but I'll stop there. Just after Thanksgiving in 2017, I recorded the interview that topped them all.

Imogene's family was one of the first to settle in Pensacola, Florida, and she worked the late shift for seventeen years at Baptist Hospital. She could get everywhere by walking. She told me about the hurricanes that have affected Pensacola, and the names of people in her neighborhood in the 1920s. That gave me pause. 1920s?

"I didn't know I'd ever reach this point in life, but I'm still here," she softly tells me.

I ask Imogene, as politely as possible, how old she is. She says she is one-hundred-one and will be one-hundred-two in February 2018. Her father was born in 1889.

"I know Pensacola real well," she says. "I love talking to people because I am a native here. We had all the names that meant something."

She tells me that she got her wheelchair ramp just before summer in 2016. A friend had received a ramp from Ray of Hope, so that was how she connected with the group. She says her daughter lives with her, to help her with day-to-day activities. She is not in a wheelchair but struggles to maintain her balance. She uses a cane while her daughter helps her down the ramp.

"When you get to be one-hundred-one years old, and trying to get around, a ramp does help," Imogene says. "It is a wonderful help in getting in and out of the house."

She says that Ray of Hope had it built in "rapid time," completed just after lunch one Saturday afternoon. This is precisely where her impassioned speech begins. I ask her about Ray of Hope performing this selfless act of kindness for her, and what that means to her in a time dominated by political and crime-ridden headlines.

"The whole world has gone crazy," she says.

The newspaper story sticking in her mind that day was already a month old, reported in October 2017, but it was so heinous that she decides to tell me about it. A three-hundred-pound woman living in Pensacola, the same town she has called home for most of her life, was charged with murder by authorities for allegedly sitting on her young cousin as punishment for misbehaving, causing the girl to die of cardiac arrest. Imogene shared the story with her granddaughter, who lives in Atlanta.

"What's the matter with these people?" she asks me.

She says that every time the newspaper comes to her house, she cringes. She takes no chances and stays home at night. You don't know what or who you will run into anymore, she says.

"People are absolutely insane," Imogene deadpans.

A short pause gives me just enough time to interject a question. I ask Imogene if today's negativity makes what Ray of Hope does that much more impressive, that much more of a blessing. She answers by telling me about her late shift working at the hospital, how a guard used to walk her and other nurses to their cars, just to be safe.

It is hard to keep people on track when you are interviewing them. I quickly learn that is a completely different task to do so with someone who is one-hundred-one years old. So, I tell Imogene that I have no more questions, that I just enjoy listening to people's stories.

She goes on to tell me, again, that she knew Pensacola well enough to walk anywhere she wanted. All of her relatives lived within walking distance of her growing up. She tells me that a new jail is being constructed nearby, something she believes won't be big enough to hold all the bad people running around the streets these days. She again brings up the article she read about the woman sitting on and killing her little cousin.

"I said, 'Dear God, what in the world is happening to people?' Lucifer is loose and is he busy."

I again take this opportunity to mention the positivity that Ray of Hope provides to her section of the world, that even though many things seem dim and grim, that group is doing right, that it is on a mission from God. She agrees.

She briefly talks about Ray of Hope again, stating that she has a tremendous horror of falling, and will not attempt to use the ramp when it is wet. She was then back to her speech, saying they -- who is they? -- built to the east side of Escambia Bay and to the north of her. The Gulf of Mexico was to the south, and commercialism is now moving west.

"Every little spot you see something going up," she says.

I tell her that I did think of another question, about the founder of Ray of Hope, Jimmy Ray. I ask her what her thoughts are on someone helping others the way he did. She tells me that she had a cousin who lived on Garden

Street, and the property right by her house was sold, and now she is worried about what will be put up there.

"We don't have any laws here that protect us from people just putting up anything," Imogene says.

How do you tell a one-hundred-one-year-old woman that she is not answering your questions, that she is not helping? You can't. You just listen, listen, and listen. You remain patient through all the extraneous information and hope for a nugget of the good stuff. I try again with a pointed question. I ask if Ray of Hope building more than five hundred wheelchair ramps surprises her. She answers about laws protecting property.

"We have to have some," she says. "You can't give Mother Nature away."

I say "Yes, ma'am," and thank her for her time. My tape recorder shows that we have talked for more than twenty-two minutes. I tell her I can't think of anything else to ask. She pauses before saying that the volunteers had two young girls with them helping build her ramp.

"If we had more people doing things like that, it would begin to help a little bit," she says.

The nugget of good information finally appears. She goes from focusing on the negativity in the world to the good stuff. She says to me that she reads the newspaper every day, which I already know. This time, however, she says that the first thing she reads are the obituaries, to check for people she knows "who have gone to the great, wonderful beyond." She hopes that there are some people left on this earth, like the Ray of Hope volunteers, who can rebuild what's left of a broken world.

"People don't know what work is," Imogene says. "That's what we've got to look at. We have to have some better people working on things and trying to get people to understand how to help people. It's sickening to think about the things that are going on."

At this point, after twenty-five minutes, I can tell I'm getting through to her. I tell Imogene that I'm trying to do my part to put out some good stories about Ray of Hope, to bring some positivity to her corner of the world.

"Let's hope it'll come soon, because every day I find new things that are happening," she says.

Imogene goes back in time in her mind. She grew up during the Great Depression, and a family member ran a restaurant in downtown Pensacola. Leftover food was taken home and divided amongst relatives. An aunt had a small farm in Cantonment, Florida, and she would fill her car to its roof with vegetables for the family. Seeing those things as a girl helped Imogene in doing nice things for others as she got older. She would have children pick blackberries and bring them to her house. She made them blackberry cobbler, which they would eat under the trees.

"Everybody helped everybody," she says. "People were willing to help each other."

She says simple acts such as those kept people together, kept them doing something worthwhile. She says that today, people want to come to the United States because they believe the sidewalks are made of gold.

"Anything worth having is worth working for," she says. "But people don't see that."

I tell Imogene that I plan to have the book done by spring or summer of 2018, and that I will surely drive to the Pensacola area with a box of books for people. I say that I will let her know when I am coming.

"Well, let's hope we don't run out of space before that happens because they're piling in here now," she says, back on her impassioned plea for city growth to slow down just a little bit.

Then, one more nugget.

"There are people that are trying to do the right thing to help each other," she says. "There are good people, if we can just find them."

I thank her one final time, especially for that last comment, and, without fail, Imogene is back talking about how things used to be, and how much different society is today.

"Well, we'll keep trying anyway," she says.

Part 3

Chapter 28: No more powerful than that

David Boyd, a longtime Ray of Hope volunteer, moved to South Carolina in June 2016 to become a congregational life minister. He finished seminary a couple months before moving. By this time, Ray of Hope had constructed more than five hundred ramps.

"It's unbelievable," Boyd says.

He is an emotional guy. Over the course of a thirty-minute phone interview, he breaks down and cries a few times while speaking about Jimmy and about helping others. His sniffling sounds like static, and the occasional silence makes me wonder if the call has been dropped due to shoddy service. He assures me that he is still on the line. Volunteering with Ray of Hope has clearly impacted his life in a profound way. He knows that the ramps have helped little boys and girls who will get use out of them for years to come. They will help parents who could not afford them, could not bear to carry their son or daughter in and out of the house several times a day. But he also knows it has helped others for six months, some significantly less, before they pass away. He knows that those ramps, the ones used for a short amount of time, provided peace for people who were coming home for the last time. It may have served as one of the last lights in a dark period for them.

"It don't get no more powerful than that," David says.

Not long after arriving in South Carolina, David attended a weeklong youth camp. It ran the week after the Fourth of July. In South Carolina, these camps go all summer long, and various church leaders attend them to develop ideas for outreach opportunities. There was not an abundance of adults there. The camp director, Matthew, approached David.

"You ever built a wheelchair ramp?" he asked.

"Yeah, I've built a couple of them," David modestly responded, knowing that he had helped build more than just a couple.

David agreed to be the team leader for building a wheelchair ramp. He then took several kids and showed them how to build a wheelchair ramp, from the first measurement to the final nail in the handrail. It took a long time, and it was stifling hot. The ramp they built together was sixty-five feet long, a massive ramp. When it was completed, Matthew told David that he hoped he would come back to the camp the next year because he knew that he would need another wheelchair ramp built. Boyd told him that he would certainly be back, that it was a way for the Ray of Hope outreach to live on in South Carolina, his new home. The whole time he worked on that huge ramp with those boys, he thought about Jimmy.

    He barely gets the words out: "It's like he's sitting there going, 'Hey, son, I told you you could do it.'"

Chapter 29: Five hundred

In June 2016, Ray of Hope completed its five hundredth ramp. What a jaw-dropping accomplishment. Five hundred times, someone in northwest Florida found out he or she was receiving a wheelchair ramp. Five hundred times, Jimmy or Ray of Hope volunteers had traveled to a home to measure for a ramp. Five hundred times, wood and nails were bought with donated money. Five hundred times, dozens of people showed up to bless others in need. Five hundred times, ramps were prayed over. Five hundred times, lives were changed.

"I just never fathomed that it would go this far," says Billy Pittman, one of Jimmy's best friends.

Billy knows that Jimmy would not want recognition for Ray of Hope.

"He would say, 'It's all for the glory of the Lord,'" he says.

David Boyd can see both sides of the amazing accomplishment. On the one hand, Woodbine United Methodist Church would be dead broke, spending money to build the ramps.

"Somehow, the Lord provided," David says.

That would not surprise Jimmy. But on the other hand, building five hundred wheelchair ramps was likely one of those accomplishments Jimmy dreamed about, like a little boy dreaming of a game-winning home run in the World Series for the New York Yankees, or a young girl yearning for a glamorous career in the fashion industry. David remembers that if a person or group wanted to honor Jimmy for his contributions to the community, he was nowhere to be found. He didn't want the attention. But if some money came in for a ramp, he would use up the little bit of energy he had to climb into the cab of a truck, sit on the tailgate, and instruct others how to build the ramp.

"But he was there," David says. "He was there. That's how much he believed in it."

Jimmy's daughter, Jessica, confidently says that her father would not be surprised by the large number of ramps that have been constructed. She says that it was his life, what he did every day.

"I think it would just be another day, another ramp, another family helped," she says. "He didn't keep up with the numbers and all that kind of stuff. I don't think he would really be all that shocked. I think he would be happy. I just don't think he would be shocked."

Jimmy's sister, Sharon Ray Glover, is not surprised either.

"I'm sure Jimmy smiles so big every time a ramp is finished," she says.

A few years after he took over Ray of Hope, Stan Holmes was to the point where he could not manage the list of people needing ramps on his own. There were many critical cases. The nonprofit had grown tenfold. He had job obligations. He just could not do it anymore. His first phone call went to Ramona, Jimmy's wife. He made the very difficult call from a lawn chair in his back yard, and he apologized profusely. Ramona was as sweet as she could be. She told him that she was considering moving from Pace, Florida, to Birmingham, Alabama, to be near her daughter. She said that one of the reasons she had stayed in Pace was because of the ministry.

One Ray of Hope volunteer talked of taking Stan's place, but that idea fell apart. Stan went to Ed Lutes and another Woodbine United Methodist Church member and told them that he was going to shut down the ministry, that he could not handle it anymore. The discussion included shutting the nonprofit organization down and giving the assets to the church.

The Ray of Hope Board of Directors met and voted three to one to keep it going. It was Lutes and another man, who left for another church shortly after the vote, that agreed to take it over. Another man later joined to help Ed run the day-to-day operations.

"They have done a phenomenal job of keeping Jimmy Ray's ministry going," Stan says.

Stan is not absent from Ray of Hope. He now attends the ramp builds as often as he can, and likely still jumps at the chance to finish the handrails. He is a volunteer, one of the many sweaty faces laboring on Saturday afternoons. He did not often keep up with how many ramps had been built. He does not believe it would shock Jimmy that a number as large as five hundred has been exceeded.

"He didn't expect, he knew, that the Lord was going to bring the money, the Lord was going to bring the people, the Lord was going to provide for this to keep it going," he says. "He just knew that it was going to work out. And it always worked out. It always did."

Stan speaks fast and somewhat erratically, as if he is in a hurry to get somewhere. He jumps around from one story to another, and he apologizes for it. It is sometimes difficult to understand when he has started a new sentence. He is a talking run-on sentence. It is clearly passion that drives this speed and need to explain, as if he has fifteen minutes to tell you an hourlong story. But talking about Jimmy's legacy gives him pause, time to gather his thoughts. He believes that if you told Jimmy his dream has produced more than five hundred wheelchair ramps free of charge, he would give you a half smile and say, "Well, why are you surprised?"

"He was the absolute picture of a servant," Stan says.

Ramona can predict better than anyone else how Jimmy would react to hundreds and hundreds of wheelchair ramps built in his name. She knew him best, of course. She, herself, never fathomed that when she and Jessica tagged along to help that there would eventually be this many wheelchair ramps. She thinks back to when Jimmy was a young man, when he was seldom motivated by others to do something big and spectacular with his life, to make a lot of money, to reach for the stars.

"It is amazing to know that someone like Jimmy, that was quiet, shy, humble, could have that kind of an effect," she says. "To know that someone like that could actually do what he did, it had to be a God thing. It just couldn't be anything else."

Ramona believes Jimmy would have never been satisfied with his passion knowing that there was one more person, one hundred more people, one thousand more people, out there in need of wheelchair ramps. He would have kept building them for as long as he could, for as many people as he could. She knows this, unequivocally. That sort of passion is not satisfied by a number. She has wondered, however, for quite some time what his thoughts would be. She comes up with only nine words.

"I wonder when we will get to six hundred."

Epilogue: Galatians

I'm no theologian.

Growing up, I avoided Sunday school when I could, using hollow excuses to try to stay at home to sleep late or watch the NFL preview shows. When I did go, I flipped disconcertingly through a thick Bible, always the last one in class to locate the verse being discussed. I didn't understand the importance.

As I got older, I found the importance, like most people do. I found it while writing this book. I found a church not even a mile from my house and began attending regularly. I took notes from the sermons and actually kept them in a small binder. I watched the online services when I was out of town or sick at home. I pulled around a candy-filled red wagon for the church's Halloween trunk or treat event, and somehow possessed enough self-control not to pocket a few Twix bars. Perhaps most importantly to me, I joined a small group of four men I had never met. I have no doubt that the coinciding of writing this book -- interviewing the poor, the lonely, the brokenhearted, the

Ray of Hope volunteers -- and finding a church home is why this project is completed today.

    The small group I joined met at the church biweekly to talk about an emailed devotional we all signed up for, and for the most part, I really enjoyed having a team of guys to connect with. We talked about job problems, daily struggles, being better men and husbands, and, of course, the Crimson Tide and the Tigers. The week after our first small group semester ended, I received the latest email devotional.

    It was titled, "Go Small to Go Big," and the Bible verse printed just beneath it was Galatians 6:10: "So then, as we have opportunity, let us do good to everyone." I had attended this small group during my busiest season of writing for this book, and that verse caught my eye. I had seen it somewhere. I dug through mounds of notes, interview transcripts, outlines, an unfinished rough draft, and wheelchair ramp specifications. I found it.

    Jimmy had printed an excerpt from F.B. Meyer's devotional book "Our Daily Walk" for a Woodbine United Methodist Church Missions and Outreach Ministry newsletter. The bold, caps-locked title was TRUE BENEFICENCE. Printed beneath that was that verse, Galatians 6:10.

That book excerpt describes Christ's command to each of us is begun with the person next to us. You do not wait to be neighbored, but you neighbor someone in need. All great work in the world, the excerpt states, is initiated not by groups, but by dedication, sacrifice and devotion of single individuals. The devotional goes on to list three methods of helping people, as instructed by the Apostle Paul:

1. The restoration of the fallen, as described in Galatians 6:1

2. The care of pastors and ministers, as described in Galatians 6:6

3. The ministry of all men, as described in Galatians 6:9-10

It was in that third method that a clear picture of Jimmy and Ray of Hope was painted in my mind. F.B. Meyer wrote, "These opportunities of doing good are always recurring, and at every turn there are those who need a helping hand. Let us bear a little of the burden of each, and especially do it for those who belong to the household of faith."

That is exactly what this nonprofit organization does. It lends a helping hand to those in need. It bears a burden for the poor and the disheartened. It provides a light in darkness, a darkness that never overcomes the light.

After finding Jimmy's missions and outreach ministry newsletter, I turned my attention back to the emailed devotional as part of my small group's study and read more from Galatians and about beneficence. The author wrote about how men often like to "go big" when they have decided to do something. He mentioned how great things can result from going big, but that mentality can also backfire. We can set our sights too high. We can get overwhelmed and stressed. We can even quit. He advised to start small. The "going big" mindset leads to a hope of grabbing a bit of glory for ourselves. Jimmy started small. He didn't start off with a truck and trailer full of lumber and power tools. He had some nails, a couple hammers, barely enough of his own money, and the help of his wife and a young daughter who toted around a plastic red hammer. He poured his heart into those wheelchair ramps, one at a time. As the nonprofit organization grew in its number of volunteers, and as its list of people in need stretched across multiple pages, he focused on one ramp, and one person, at a time. When recognition came his way, like the time a community group wanted to honor him at some swanky dinner, he was nowhere to be found. He was likely drawing up specifications for the next ramp or out making phone calls for donations. True beneficence.

    Each emailed devotional is concluded with a call to action, titled, "Okay, so what do we do?" This particular devotional, teaching on Galatians, said this: "Look around, today and tomorrow, for people in need. People are hurting, people right around you. 'Go to the lost, confused people right here in the neighborhood' (Matthew 10:5-8). Pick one person and blow them away with some help."

    Amen.

Also by the Author

Trussville, Alabama: A Brief History

Deep Green

Heart of the Plate

Valley Road: Uplifting Stories from Down South

Made in United States
Orlando, FL
20 June 2024

48071454R00093